Praise for *Buying Happiness*

Plenty of books discuss building wealth. Not enough discuss using that wealth to build a great life. Kate's book *Buying Happiness* is a timely reminder of why we invest. Money is not the end in itself. Kate reminds us it is a tool to unlock choice, freedom and to help us build the life we want to live.

Alec Renehan, co-founder of Equity Mates

Buying Happiness is a meaningful contribution to the personal finance conversation, teaching the important fusion between planning for your future and enjoying the journey to get there.

Natasha Etschmann, personal finance educator @tashinvests and host of the *Get Rich Slow Club* podcast

This book is not just an essential financial roadmap, but a philosophical guide, helping us reorient our goals and priorities. Kate teaches us to not only invest our money wisely, but also to invest our time, the one resource we cannot earn back, in a meaningful and fulfilling way.

Glen James, creator and host of the *my millennial money* podcast

A fresh, holistic take on investing like none other.

Simran Kaur, author of *Girls That Invest*

Kate Campbell's *Buying Happiness* is a beautifully written personal finance book that helps you value the things that give you true happiness. Kate's book makes you focus on what you value, what you want and the time you have to achieve the happiness you deserve now and throughout your life.

Evan Lucas, author of *Mind over Money*, Head of Strategy at InvestSMART and financial media personality

Buying Happiness

Learn to invest your time and money better

Kate Campbell

MACMILLAN

To my parents, Susan and David,
for encouraging me to take risks as a child
and, more importantly, make mistakes.

First published in 2023 by Major Street Publishing Pty Ltd

First published in India 2024 by Macmillan
an imprint of Pan Macmillan Publishing India Private Limited
707 Kailash Building
26 K. G. Marg, New Delhi 110001
www.panmacmillan.co.in

Pan Macmillan, The Smithson, 6 Briset Street, Farringdon, London EC1M 5NR
Associated companies throughout the world
www.panmacmillan.com

ISBN 978-93-6113-511-8

1 3 5 7 9 8 6 4 2

Internal design by Production Works
Printed and bound in India by Thomson Press India Ltd.

Contents

Foreword

Are you *sure* this is a good idea?

That was my first thought when Kate said, 'Owen, I want to write a book.'

Over 90,000 Australians already tune into the *Australian Finance Podcast* to hear Kate speak with some of the world's leaders in finance about money, investing and how to design an ideal life. So, naturally, my gut instinct was, 'Are you sure you want to commit to writing a book when you're already doing so much? You're already helping tens of thousands of families across the country and throughout the world.' However, over the years I've known Kate, I've watched her grow and grow and grow to become one of the most influential women in Australian finance. I thought, if anyone could do it, she could – and do it well.

So, we decided to sit down and properly talk it through. What would she write about? What would she like to research? How could she help people even more than she already did? Then we studied the data and found that '8 ways to buy happiness: Rethinking how we spend our money' was one of the most popular *Australian Finance Podcast* episodes ever. The path was clear. It had to be a book about behavioural finance and about helping people use money *intentionally* to build happiness.

Now, after hundreds of episodes, thousands of hours of planning, research and practice, and countless discussions with experts in Australia and around the world, it all comes together in a book – *Buying Happiness* – designed to help you do just that: stop, reflect, recharge and start using money to improve your life.

Far too many people think, 'I can't be wealthy. I'm not smart enough.' Or, 'I don't have enough money.' Or, 'It's too scary.' Or, 'Isn't that like gambling?' These types of limiting beliefs might seem true to you now, but this book will prove that so much of what you've been taught about money simply isn't right.

You *can* do it. You *can* live a life where you don't worry about money: a life where you have everything you need *and* everything you want.

In *Buying Happiness*, Kate distils the best bits of what others have already figured out about using money to increase your happiness. After a crash course in money and laying your foundations, Kate explores techniques, strategies and methods to help you find your own answers to your real money problems and plan for the future. On top of this, she's taken the Rask community's feedback and ideas to showcase what truly matters to us all and included this at the back of this book and online at buyinghappiness.com.au.

My biggest takeaway from *Buying Happiness* is that forgiving yourself is an essential step to improving your happiness. Once you do this, you will realise – as I did – that it's good to experiment with money, even if some is lost along the way. It's important to make mistakes, so long as you learn as you go. It's crucial to take the risks you've always wanted to take, provided you know what they are. And, perhaps most important of all, it's okay to have regrets.

These are all signs that you're on the path to discovering what makes you happy – and learning to be good with your money will help you do that.

Owen Rask
Founder of Rask and host of the *Australian Finance Podcast*

Introduction

What does it mean to be happy? 'Happiness' is an interesting word, one that I believe everyone gets to define for themselves. From my perspective, it's a by-product of a well-lived life, not a destination. In *Happiness: A Very Short Introduction*, Daniel Haybron recommends that we 'give up the idea that any single account of happiness can capture everything we use the word to talk about'. People use many words to describe happiness, such as 'satisfaction', 'wellbeing', 'fulfilment' and 'contentment', but I'd like to add a few more – especially in the context of money.

Happiness is freedom. It's the ability to make choices and know when you have enough. It's about being satisfied with life right now, while still growing as a person. It's about not postponing your life to a future date. It's piecing together a tapestry of small moments that compound over time to form a good life – and that, in my view, is a lifelong journey.

In *Flourish*, Antonia Case points out that 'one does not stumble on a good life, it has to be actively managed'. This book is about using the resources at your disposal, specifically time and money, to build a good life – a happy life. While happiness can't be bottled up and purchased at a store, by taking control of your finances and thinking a little more deeply about the way you use your resources, you can improve your life.

Money, time and happiness

Money is a tool that you get to choose how you wield. While having more money won't solve all your problems, you can certainly use it to smooth the road ahead and achieve your goals. The more you learn about your money story and the better you manage your finances, the more choice you'll have – because money gives you the freedom to choose.

Whether you want to change careers, spend more time with family or travel in Europe for six months, money is a tool that can make your dream viable. To give yourself those options, however, you have to take that first step. That could look like taking a glance at your spending for the first time, having a conversation about your current savings goals with a friend, or investing your first $5. We'll do all this and more in the next ten chapters.

It's not just about money, though. Your time is another valuable asset to be spent, saved and invested with intention. It's a finite resource with a powerful effect on happiness, so it's important to consider how you can use your time in a way that feels most valuable to you – remembering that this will be unique to every individual, and will likely change throughout your life. Although you can't deposit your time in a bank account, you can create space in your days – right now and in the future – to spend your time in more meaningful ways (be that travelling, spending more time with family or even retiring early).

This book is ultimately about the choices you can make in life and supporting you to make them from a position of strength. It's a guide to using the time and money at your disposal to increase your happiness. The central idea is that if you spend, save and invest both your time and your money better, you'll have access to more of it. If you then use these additional resources to make intentional decisions about the way you spend your life, you'll be on a good path to happiness.

You can do this

Many people avoid getting on top of their finances because they think money is hard, but it doesn't have to be. As you'll discover in reading this book, a simple system can set you up for a lifetime of choices. You don't need a qualification to manage your own finances well, but you do need to start with some foundations. First up, it's important to educate yourself. This builds your confidence to make positive decisions for your financial future. By opening this book you're taking the perfect first step. It's also essential to be patient. Sorting out your finances isn't an overnight process and will take time. You need to start planting the seeds of the trees you'll sit under in the years to come. Finally, I urge you to be kind to yourself during this big (but essential) learning journey. Many people beat themselves up for not knowing about this 'money stuff' already, but it's much more important to focus on the opportunity in front of you to change your money story.

Please be kind to yourself on your money journey. Try not to get stuck comparing yourself with friends and family who are a few steps ahead of you. At times it will feel confusing and challenging, but I encourage you to push through those feelings because there's a lot to look forward to on the other side.

Using this book

In this book I share so much of what I've learnt as a financial educator and podcast host, funnelling everything I've gathered from experts over the years into the one resource. I've set out the ten major focus areas into ten different chapters, so you can easily jump into the topic that's a priority for you at any particular moment.

The first two chapters lay the essential foundations of your money journey, covering paying off high-interest debt, building an emergency fund, understanding your current financial position, budgeting and setting goals according to your values and priorities. Chapters 3 and 4 invite you to look inwards and support you to build a healthy money mindset, manage financial regrets and avoid common behavioural traps along the way. Then in chapter 5 it's time to discuss why it can be so difficult to talk about money and work through some strategies to manage vulnerable money conversations. The early chapters of this book are about giving you the tools you need to make financial decisions from a position of strength.

Chapter 6 explores the connection between time and money, suggesting ways of maintaining balance and enjoying the present (even when working towards big financial goals) by using your time more intentionally. Then in chapter 7 you'll be challenged to think deeply about how you can incorporate research-based methods of using money to buy happiness – now and in the future. Chapter 8 is all about getting started on your investment journey and making your money work for you. You'll learn about the magic of compound interest, open a brokerage account, invest your first $5 and automate your wealth-building journey. In chapter 9 you'll explore how risk affects your life as an investor and discuss how to take healthy risks and manage the common fear of making mistakes. Finally, in chapter 10, you'll pull together everything you know about your money, your time and what makes you happy to explore the concept of financial independence and what achieving that dream could look like for you.

To help you apply everything you learn in this book to your own life, I've included plenty of exercises (indicated by this little pencil), conversation starters, and tips and tricks that you can use right now. As we'll sometimes be working through some new or tricky ideas, I've also collected the essential takeaways in a TL;DR (too long; didn't read) summary at the end of each chapter.

Five key ideas

As you work through this book, you'll also see some key ideas pop up again and again. I'll walk you through them now to give you a head start.

It's your money. It might not seem like it right now, but you have a lot more choices about how you earn, spend, save and invest your money than you realise. By sorting out your financial foundations, you'll feel more in control of your financial future. Remember, this is your money journey and you get to choose the destination.

Talking about money is okay. It's not always fun and easy, but there's a huge benefit to having conversations about money at any age. Be the person to kick off the conversations in your own community and don't get discouraged if not everyone is open to it (research shows it's one of our least favourite topics of conversation). Most importantly, listen without judgement during these vulnerable moments.

You can buy happiness. The experts have spoken; there are many ways you can use your time and money to increase your happiness. The first step is being aware of where your time and money are currently being spent, and then adjusting your actions to get the most out of your resources.

Take small actions, lots of times. When it comes to sorting out your finances and starting to invest, it's not all or nothing. I encourage you to remember that you can start small, but start *now* – and take regular action. Your confidence is built through the actions you take.

Take healthy risks. Many of the things that make us happiest today began with taking a risk – be that a career, partner, business or hobby. We need to see taking healthy risks as a positive part of the journey to building wealth. Plus, it turns out taking risks actually makes us happier; how great is that!

Bookmark this page so you can come back to these five key ideas whenever you feel uncertain or need reminding of what's important on your financial journey.

My community and crowdsourcing happiness

I've hosted the *Australian Finance Podcast* with investment analyst Owen Rask since the start of 2019 – and it has been a journey! We now talk to over 80,000 unique listeners a month who want to learn the skills to supercharge their own financial future. If I reference 'the podcast' or 'the show', this is what I'm talking about. If I mention my community, I'm talking about the people who listen to the show, take our investing courses on Rask Education or engage with Rask Australia on social media.

I've learned so much from this community over the years, so when I started writing this book I invited members to share with me how they've used their time and money to buy happiness. You can find highlights from their responses in 'Crowdsourced happiness' at the end of the book, and I share many more online at buyinghappiness.com.au. I hope these real examples inspire you to find your own happiness along the way.

Let's begin

I got lucky. I figured out what makes me happy in my 20s and I'm actively designing my finances around the life I want to live. I've had the opportunity to speak with experts in their fields about everything from investing my time better to achieving financial freedom. But we don't all start our money journeys at the same point. This book discusses long-term thinking, goal-setting and taking action – and that's not going to be easy for everyone.

I encourage you to be kind and patient with yourself during this journey. Don't judge yourself against someone else's timeline, but *do* get started today. I know from experience that it's all well and good learning as much as you can about your money, but if you don't take any action, you'll look back in ten years' time and wonder why.

If this is the first money book you've ever read, I can't wait to help you get started. If you've been on your finance journey for a while, I look forward to sharing insights that'll add value to your life.

1

Finding your feet

Pay off high-interest debt and build your emergency fund

The journey of a thousand miles begins with one step.
Lao Tzu

If I've learnt anything on my money journey, it's the importance of getting the foundations right. Many of the mistakes we end up making with money happen because we jump into the deep end without first learning to swim. The first two chapters cover the essential foundations of your money journey. Though it might be uncomfortable or difficult, it's essential you stick with me if you haven't already taken those first steps. Happiness costs time and money. It requires you to put in the work – and this is that work.

If you're beginning your finance journey a little later in life, please know that you are not alone. Whatever lessons you've learnt, missteps you've made or regrets you have about not sorting this all out earlier can be used as fuel for your next steps. Forgive yourself for the decisions you made when you had less information and fewer resources.

My mum has always told me to look for kindness in the people I form relationships with, and that has always served me well.

It's important to be kind to yourself, too. You deserve the opportunity to learn about money and take steps to improve your financial future. It's the actions you take from this day forward that matter.

As we're all starting this journey at different points, some parts of this book may be more relevant to you than other parts, and I'm a big believer in gathering the information you need when you need it. You don't have to read every chapter or even read the chapters in order. Life's too short for that.

For example, feel free to skip ahead to chapter 3 where we talk about your money mindset if you tick all the following boxes:

- You've paid off your high-interest debts (such as car loans, personal loans and credit cards).
- You've set up an emergency fund (approximately 3–6 months of expenses set aside in a savings account).
- You know what your income is and where your money is going each month.
- You've set some money goals and have a solid plan to reach them.

However, if that's not you, keep reading. In this chapter we're going to work through paying off high-interest debts and setting up an emergency fund, then in the next chapter we'll figure out your current financial position and get started on goal-setting. These are all important steps in increasing your overall feelings of financial wellbeing.

Sound good? Let's jump in!

Paying off high-interest debt

Paul struggled to find a full-time job after finishing university, but the bills he faced after moving out started to pile up. Thankfully (or so he thought at the time), the bank was more than happy to send him a credit card with a $10,000 limit, which he eventually used to pay for everything. He'd maxed out the card after a few years and, while he made the minimum repayments each month, he wasn't too worried about paying off the debt. When Paul turned 30 he started to get his financial affairs in order and finally looked into paying off his credit card. However, when he asked the bank how much was left to pay, he was shocked to find out he owed them a lot more than $10,000. How on earth did Paul end up there?

There's a common misconception that people who end up in debt made bad choices, tried to start a business that didn't work out or lashed out on some luxurious overseas holiday. These things all happen, but the truth is that it's generally just a build-up of small purchases over time: a medical expense here, a grocery bill there. Mix in a very profitable line of credit 'kindly' offered by a bank – and boom. Suddenly those small expenses have snowballed into something unrecognisable.

I'll discuss how compound interest can help you build wealth later in this book, but first let's discuss how it works against you when you're the one paying it. If you had a $10,000 credit card debt (like Paul did before it grew), were being charged 20 per cent a year in interest by your bank and made only the minimum repayment of around $200 (2 per cent of the loan balance) each month, it would take you over 60 years to pay it off. Worse still, over the life of the loan you'd end up paying the bank over $40,000 in interest alone! Compare this to making higher repayments of around $500 each month, which would clear your debt in approximately two years, and you'd only pay $2000 in interest over the life of the loan.

Getting out of high-interest debt is a hard but important part of sorting out your finances. It'll build your financial confidence, help you pay less in interest over the life of your loan and put more money in your pocket for your own goals. Plus, paying off these debts will take a whole heap of stress off your plate. I'm focusing on debts like loans from friends and family, buy now pay later (BNPL), payday loans, car loans, personal loans and credit cards because they can be harmful to relationships, get you into a cycle of debt or charge you a higher interest rate than you could earn by saving or investing instead.

This is just a general guide and ultimately you will need to decide what your financial priorities are.

If you want to speed up the process and get your lender off your back, you'll need to consider making more than the minimum repayments each month. So how do you get started? Whether you're trying to pay off your BNPL purchases, take control of your car loan or reduce your credit card debt, here are five steps to follow that can make the tough process of figuring out your high-interest debts a little simpler.

Step 1: Write everything down

This first step is tough, but it's necessary. Find all your paperwork, emails and logins for any current debts in your name and write them down. Then hunt down details like the size of each debt, who you need to make repayments to, how fast the debt is growing (the yearly interest rate), when the debt is due, the minimum repayments and so on. All of this data will help you make more informed decisions in step 3.

Step 2: Identify what led you to this point

Before you begin this step, I want to stress that this isn't about being hard on yourself and allocating blame. Rather, it's about being curious about the circumstances, choices and purchases that led you to being in debt. If you skip this step, you may find yourself repeating certain behaviours and ending up in debt again, which is definitely something you want to avoid.

Take the information you assembled in step 1 and try to answer each of these questions:

- When did this debt start?
- What was happening in your life when you took on this debt (took out the loan, applied for the credit card)?

- Where was most of the money spent? (This will be easier for something like a car loan and a little more work for a credit card balance you've been carrying for years.)
- Are you still adding to the debt on a regular basis? (This is important because until you're able to balance out your monthly income and expenses, it will be very difficult to make a lot of progress.)
- Who have you told about your debt?
- How much do you want to be debt free? What sacrifices are you prepared to make to pay everything off?

These questions may be challenging to answer, but this opportunity to reflect on your path into debt will help you create a more informed plan in step 3 to move in a different (and better) direction. There's a quote that resonates here from the late Maya Angelou: 'Do the best you can until you know better. Then when you know better, do better.' The better you understand yourself and the way you manage your money, the stronger the position from which you'll be able to make financial decisions going forwards.

Step 3: Make a plan

If you're relying on a credit card or personal loan because your monthly expenses are greater than your monthly income, it's important to focus on this first. Before you can make progress towards paying off your debt, you'll need to find a way to flip these numbers around so that your income is greater than your expenses. Before you make a plan to pay off your debt, it's important to stop adding to it. Here are a few preliminary ideas:

- If you're struggling to pay your bills, call your bank or service provider and ask to speak to their financial hardship team. They may be able to help you set up a payment plan or offer other short-term solutions.

- Run through your bank statements over the past three months and cancel any non-essential expenses (including any subscriptions that have been running in the background).
- Decide if there are any areas in your spending that you can cut back on. For example, until you have your debt under control, catch-ups with friends could be walks or homemade dinners instead of nights out.
- Find any items around the house you haven't used recently that can be sold on Gumtree or Facebook Marketplace.
- Are there any ways you can earn some extra money right now? This might include taking on extra shifts, doing gig work after hours or finding a second job. For example, I spoke to an Uber driver who was driving for two hours each day outside of his 9–5 to pay down his debt and get a handle on his finances.

Once you've found a way to ensure your income is greater than your expenses, it's time to think about how to pay off your debt. Here are my suggestions:

- Work out the order in which you want to pay your debts off. You might consider paying off the highest-interest debt first, for example. Some people prefer the snowball method, where you pay off debts from smallest dollar value to largest to keep you motivated.
- Set out a realistic repayment schedule. What's left in your bank account at the end of the month? How much of this can you put towards making extra repayments? Write down a realistic plan, including the additional fortnightly or monthly repayments you can make, being very clear on where the money is going, how often you'll make the repayments and when the debt will be paid off by. If you can automate these payments to leave your bank account each month without even thinking about it, even better!
- Decrease your expenses as much as possible while still providing yourself with flexibility on your debt repayment journey.

What are some bigger moves you can make to reduce your expenses? Things might be really tight right now, but if paying off your debt is a priority, could you sell your car and buy a cheaper second-hand one, move into a share house or back home, or replace higher-cost activities with lower-cost options? For example, could you skip the bigger holiday and opt for a local road trip, or ask family to run a Secret Santa this year rather than having to buy everyone gifts?

- Explore longer-term ways to increase your income, such as building a case for a pay rise, taking an after-hours course that will help you to move into a higher-paying industry or starting a side hustle.
- Remember to track how you're progressing on a regular basis and adjust your plan if necessary. This plan should be something that works *with* you, not *against* you. Also, be sure to find ways to create and celebrate milestones along the way, especially if your debt is quite large, to stay motivated and acknowledge your progress.

Paying off debt can be a tough journey, but it's a foundational stage in taking back control of your finances. Plus, it'll get you one step closer to *making* interest on your money, not paying it, and who doesn't like the sound of that?

Step 4: Get help

If this is all feeling a little overwhelming, consider asking someone you trust to help you make a plan and check in with you on a regular basis. Paying off debt can feel very lonely, but you're definitely not alone. Many online groups focused on becoming debt-free, where people encourage and support each other through the journey, have sprung up on a range of different platforms. The sense of community these groups offer can be valuable.

Many countries also have financial counsellors or advisers who are qualified to help you pay off debts and deal with banks and service providers. In Australia, the National Debt Helpline is an excellent resource where you can speak to a financial counsellor confidentially and for free. They can provide you with valuable support and guidance on your journey. Another helpful resource is the Financial Rights Legal Centre, which can help you understand your legal rights in relation to financial debts and disputes. Asking for help is okay; in my books, it's a sign of strength.

Step 5: Stay motivated

Paying off debt isn't an overnight journey, and for many people, getting the lender off their back will take a few years. It can be hard to stay motivated, so try to acknowledge the small wins, and be kind to yourself if you can't stick to your plan every month. It may need to be adjusted, or you might just need a quick reset before you're back on track.

Even though there are just a few steps here, while you're doing the hard work of paying off your debt, the process can feel anything but simple. To help you keep your head up when things are tough, I encourage you to celebrate whenever you hit a milestone and focus on the positives of your journey to becoming debt-free. For example, consider the great money habits you're building on the way. Consistently putting money aside in your budget to pay off debt every month is a skill that can be directly transferred to saving and investing in the future. Best of all, when you do reach your goal of being debt-free, you'll have accomplished a huge feat and should be really proud of yourself.

Finally, I really encourage you to use this time wisely and learn as much as you can about your finances and investing during this process. This will put you in the best possible position to change the direction of your financial future.

A note on BNPL

Borrowing money and being in debt is a tale as old as time, with stories about lenders and loans dating back to 2000 BCE. These days we've got more options than ever before when it comes to borrowing money, and brands are using the research of experts in consumer behaviour against us. They know exactly which buttons to push, colours to use and cookies to track to convince us that we need that item – and we need it now. Enter buy now pay later (BNPL) services, the modern-day consumer's best friend (as they would have you believe).

If you're not familiar, BNPL allows consumers to access goods and services by paying only a small portion of the total cost upfront, with the rest to be paid in instalments over the months that follow. Plus, for many of these services, the merchant (not you) pays the upfront costs. Sounds great, right? Maybe not. Research from BNPL platforms themselves suggests that consumers spend more when using BNPL at the check-out than they do if they have to save up for their purchase prior to making it. One company tells business owners that by offering their service at check-out, they will increase the average order value by up to 18 per cent, while another touts a 41 per cent increase in average order value. While that might sound great for a business, it's not so good for you. Many consumers also use multiple BNPL platforms at once, and what originally seemed like a helpful tool at check-out can quickly snowball into an ongoing cycle of debt.

For all of these reasons, it might be a good idea to avoid using BNPL if you can. Plus, as you'll learn in chapter 7, there's a lot of research that shows saving up for and anticipating a purchase actually increases your overall levels of satisfaction.

Building your emergency fund

You know those weeks when everything goes wrong and you can't seem to keep your head above water? You're looking at your bank account and you know there's not enough in there to cover everything, so you pull out that credit card you've been keeping for emergencies and resign yourself to going back into debt for the next year or two. But what if you didn't have to go into debt? What if you had money set aside for a situation exactly like this?

This is what your emergency fund is for. It's money you put aside specifically for the challenges life loves to throw at you, challenges that you can't really plan for, like a family emergency. It's also the money that gives you the financial breathing room to leave a toxic job, a bad relationship or unsafe situation. This is one of the areas of finance I am most passionate about, because while investing is great, having the power to make decisions from a position of financial strength is even better.

So, how much do you need? There are many different ways to cut this cake, but a good place to start is anywhere from three months to six months of basic living expenses – and having that money stashed in a high-interest savings account (so you can access it when you need to) is important too. If you have a good (and financially-secure) family support system, work in a highly sought-after role or have multiple sources of income, you might be completely comfortable with a smaller amount in your emergency fund. On the other hand, if nobody can support you if something bad happens, you're financially responsible for other people or you work in an industry where it could be difficult to secure your next role, you might be more comfortable knowing you've got a bigger safety net.

My mum's had breast cancer twice, and there's always that thought at the back of my mind that it could come back for a third time. If this ever happens, and I really hope with all my heart that it doesn't, I want to be able to drop everything to spend quality time with her. That could be flights, unpaid leave from work or a family holiday – and all those things cost money. That's why having a larger emergency fund is so important to me, even though I could probably get by with much less. I don't want my choices in a challenging situation to be dictated by my finances.

If you think about it, you've probably also faced some challenging situations in which having a break-glass-in-case-of-emergency account would've come in handy. Have I convinced you that you need an emergency fund yet? If so, it's time to get cracking.

Step 1: Open your emergency account

First things first, open a completely separate bank account that isn't directly linked to a spending account and label it as your dedicated emergency fund. Ideally this will be a high-interest savings account that won't charge you account-keeping or withdrawal fees and allows you to access the money quickly. This account will be used solely for your emergency fund, so you'll have to practise self-restraint and access it only for emergency situations.

Step 2: Set a goal and budget for it

Your next step is to work out how much you'll need in your emergency fund. Consider your needs and your current financial situation. Once you've got a number in mind, you'll need to make room in your monthly budget for it (unless you've already got the money available to move into your emergency fund straight away). Here's an example:

> *I've determined that I need around $3000 to feel comfortable, and I've worked out that I can reach that goal by transferring $250 into my emergency fund each month for the next 12 months. If I can also take on some extra work during the holidays or sell some items around the house to speed up the process, that would be a bonus!*

Remember, whether it's $500 or six months' living expenses, you need to work out the appropriate emergency fund goal for you. For example, if you have competing priorities or you're currently paying off debt, it may be better to start by putting aside just one month of living expenses and committing to building up your emergency fund over time.

Step 3: Set up automatic payments

Once you've worked out how much you want to move into your emergency fund each month, set up an automatic payment depositing the planned amount of money into your emergency fund from the account you receive your salary into. If that's not an option, put a recurring calendar event in your diary that reminds you to move money across to your emergency fund.

This step draws on US financial educator Ramit Sethi's automation-centred approach to building wealth and security. This is how he describes the benefits of automating aspects of personal finance:

> *By setting up a bulletproof personal finance system, you can start to dominate your finances by having your system passively do the right thing for you, leaving you to focus on the things that really matter.*

So, put your plan on autopilot and move onto the next step!

Step 4: Be consistent

The key thing to keep in mind is that you need to be consistent with building your emergency fund. It may take a few years for you to set up your emergency fund, and you may even need to use it before you reach your goal, but don't be discouraged. After getting started, continuing to add to your fund until you reach your goal is the most important part of this process – even if it feels like you're not really getting anywhere. If you have any unexpected windfalls, such as a tax refund or a bonus, consider them good opportunities to boost your emergency fund.

Step 5: Use – and replenish – your emergency fund

Finally, once you've got your emergency fund in place, or at least in progress, don't be afraid to use that money if something unexpected happens. That's what it's there for! Just think of it as your personal parachute that you can open in case of emergency. If you do have to use your emergency fund, start repairing it straight away!

That's great in theory, but it can be a bit harder in practice. If you have difficulty actually spending money after you've saved up for something, you may find it challenging to use your emergency fund when you need it. My suggestion to you here is to reflect on what kind of situations would warrant breaking the glass, so to speak, and writing them down. This ties into your values, so it'll look different to everyone, but the list could include things like flying interstate for a funeral, taking time off work to support a friend having a tough time or getting an urgent car repair. Remember that this money has been put aside by past-you to support future-you in tough times and using that support is okay!

It's true that replenishing an emergency fund that you've worked hard to build can feel a little disheartening, but don't let that stop you. You might need to take a short break and have a breather before you get going again; however, you'll get there – and this time you're not starting from scratch. Not only have you already got your emergency fund account set up and know how much you need, but you've also built the skills and discipline required to reach your goal again. So, if this is you, remember you've got this!

TL;DR

Getting the foundations right is important. Though what you've read in this chapter mightn't sound that exciting, sorting out the building blocks of your finances gives you bang for your buck. If buying happiness is your goal, paying off debt and building your emergency fund are essential steps on your journey.

- Building your financial foundations is an important part of your journey. Don't skip it.

- People usually end up in debt because of many small purchases that build up over time. It can take time to unpack this, and more time still to actually pay off the debt, but it's important to reflect on what caused your debt to avoid repeating the pattern.
- Paying off debt is hard and takes resources, but that doesn't mean you shouldn't do it. Find people to support you on your journey and reach out if you need help.
- You need a break-glass-in-case-of-emergency account. Having 3–6 months of expenses in a high-interest savings account is a key factor in increasing your financial wellness levels.
- You'll probably have to use your emergency fund at some point – and that's okay! Just remember to breathe, deal with the situation at hand and then, when you're ready, start filling it back up again.

2

Feeling financially confident

Understand your financial position, start budgeting and set money goals

I think the best way to have confidence is not to allow everyone else's insecurities to be your own.
Jessie J

We get so caught up in the busyness of life that years can easily slip by before we check in with our finances, but today we're going to change that. Now that we've found our financial footing, how do we start feeling financially confident? This chapter is all about setting up your finances so you can start making decisions about your life from a position of strength. We're going to take a closer look at your current financial position (which means getting crystal clear on things such as income, expenses, assets and liabilities), creating a budget that works and starting to set financial goals that align with your values.

Your financial position

I like to think of my life as a business. I've got income and expenses, assets and liabilities, and I'm effectively wearing the hats of CEO, operations manager, marketing, human resources, finance and tech support. A business requires work. It needs a budget. It needs goals, performance reviews, an annual report, a board of directors and, hopefully, at least one customer.

I want you to imagine now that you're a business. You have income from your clients (your day job) who expect a service in return. Maybe your business has other products or services (this could include any side hustles, freelancing or dividends) that bring in some extra income. Then your business has expenses (for example, rent, groceries, internet) that have to be dealt with on a weekly or monthly basis. Your business may also have assets (shares, property, cash) or debts (car loan, credit card, mortgage) on its balance sheet. For the business to remain financially viable, the income needs to be greater than the expenses. (No, you're not getting any venture capital or shark tank money in this scenario.)

Considering all of these factors, is your business currently operating in a healthy manner, or is it running at a loss? You can figure this out by looking at your assets, liabilities, income and expenses. A clear understanding of your current financial position will help you to gain control over your money, just like a business.

Work out your income and expenses

Now that you're in the CEO's hot seat, it's time to get on top of all the money coming into and going out of your bank accounts. Sorting this out is important because, if you want to start spending your money to buy happiness, you first need to check in and get a status update.

✎ This may take a bit of time if you've never done it before, but knowing your numbers is a critical step in your personal finance journey. Get out a piece of paper or bring up your spreadsheet and make a list for each of the following:

1. **Your income.** This will be easy if you have just one full-time job, but it might be a little more difficult if you're working multiple roles or you're employed on a casual basis. Look through the

income you've received over the last six months and come up with an average monthly figure.

2. **Your expenses.** This is the fun bit! Figure out your average monthly spending over the past six months. Your bank may allow you to export your transaction history, or you may be able to use in-app budgeting features to get this figure.

Now you've got an understanding of your average income and expenses, you're in a good position to work out how much you currently save each month. Use the following equation to work this out:

your average monthly income – your average monthly expenses = your average monthly surplus or shortfall

You've now either got a positive or negative number staring at you. I want you to consider the following:

- If you have a positive number, a surplus, how are you currently using that money? Is it sitting in a bank account, have you saved it for a specific goal, have you used it to pay down debt or have you invested it?
- If you have a negative number, a shortfall, are you using debt or your savings to bridge the gap between your income and expenses? What changes could you make that could help you have some money left over at the end of each month?

Now you're starting to get an idea of where you're currently sitting financially. It's best to run through this process on a monthly basis to make sure you're tracking towards your goals. In a company, a CFO/bookkeeper would prepare the financials each month, but since you're the business here, it's up to you to do this.

Work out your net worth

Your net worth gives you an indication of where you're currently sitting financially and helps you make more informed money decisions, especially when it comes to big goals like taking time off work, a world trip or retirement. It's just one tool in your kit to see how you're progressing towards your goals.

✎ Calculating net worth itself is fairly simple. Start by making a list of all your assets (that'll be cash, investments and anything else you believe holds value if you sold it today) and adding it up. I wouldn't worry too much about including lower-value items like electronics; keep things quick and simple. Then repeat the process with any liabilities you have (for example, credit cards, mortgages and money you owe your friend). I like to do this in a spreadsheet to track these numbers over time, but if writing it down or just using the notes app on your phone makes things easier, go for it.

Once you've got everything tallied up, complete the following calculation:

your assets – your liabilities = your net worth

Done! That wasn't so hard, was it?

This could end up being a negative number and that's completely okay. This is all about collecting data to make better-informed financial decisions. I like to think of my net worth as a bird's-eye view of my financial life. I can get a general sense of whether I'm moving in a positive direction over time by looking at how my net worth is changing. Try to look at these numbers like a scientist in a lab and take this opportunity to check in with your assets and liabilities. This might be a reminder, for example, that you need to focus more on paying down debt, rebuilding your emergency fund or investing more regularly.

That said, it's important not to tie your money goals to your net worth. When you start investing (which we'll discuss in greater detail in chapter 8), your balance will fluctuate daily and your net worth will change due to factors outside your direct control. Just remember: your net worth does not equal your self-worth. A wonderful, well-lived life is measured by much more than dollars and cents.

A note on comparison

Have you ever wondered about how much money your friend, a neighbour or that influencer you follow really has? While it's a bit of fun to see the empires that other people are – or aren't – building, in this book I really want to focus on you. It can be so easy to get distracted by someone else's apparent wealth and assume their life must be wonderful. However, many of our fundamental human problems, insecurities and worries don't disappear overnight with money. Sure, these people might be able to afford the best trainer, hairdresser and personal chef that money can buy, but if they're unhappy with their lives and their relationships, no amount of money is going to fix that.

I say this especially to those at the beginning of their financial journey who are looking at others – friends, colleagues, family or even celebrities – with significantly more established financial portfolios. It can be disheartening when you're just starting out to see someone the same age as you (or younger) with everything 'sorted out', or to find out that a colleague with similar earning capacity is ten years ahead of you on their financial journey. Making comparisons like these often leads to the feeling that you've fallen behind, which is hardly going to encourage you on your journey. Sometimes we can get so swept up in the successes and failures of those around us that we can forget to get our own financial house in order.

Financial comparison can sneak up on us at any point during our money journey. From the conversations I've had with experts on the *Australian Finance Podcast* over the years, it's a tricky one to eliminate completely. The best strategy I've found is to get clear on my own financial goals and take regular action to work towards them. You don't need to match anyone else's goals or timeline – only your own.

With that out of the way, let's jump into an actionable way you can focus on your own financial future.

Budgeting like a boss

You've collected all this data. Now you're ready to turn it into something useful. I know many people feel a lot of resistance about budgeting and that the whole thing feels like homework for adults, but hear me out. A budget is just a plan to allocate the financial resources you have at your disposal. The more actively you use a budget, the more success you'll have later on when you explore how to use your resources in a more meaningful way.

The central principle of personal finance is to spend less than you earn and save or invest the difference. I'm going to suggest three different budgeting methods you can try. They all look different to the typical budget in which a set amount of money is allocated to every single category of spending (say, $400 on groceries or $100 on entertainment). While that method can work well for some people, it often ends up feeling restrictive and hard to manage and does spending ever run perfectly to plan?!

The 50/30/20 budget

If you're unsure where to start, the 50/30/20 budget might be a good method for you. You worked out your income and expenses earlier in this chapter, but now you'll want to break this down into the following three categories:

- **Fixed expenses ('needs')** – how much do you currently spend each month on the essentials like rent, electricity and groceries?
- **Chosen expenses ('wants')** – how much do you ideally want to spend each month on the things that make life great like meals with friends, streaming services and a weekend away?
- **Future-you money (financial goals)** – how much do you ideally want to allocate each month for paying off debt, working towards savings goals or investing?

The basic principle is that your needs, wants and financial goals are allocated 50 per cent, 30 per cent and 20 per cent of your income respectively. 'Needs' are loosely defined as necessary costs for you to live, such as a roof over your head, food, electricity, hot water, transportation, credit card and loan repayments and so on. 'Wants', on the other hand, includes all those things that you enjoy but, let's face it, could go without if you had to. Things like entertainment and social outings fall into the 'wants' category. Financial goals are completely dependent on what's a priority for you and your life. For example, your goal could be debt reduction, saving for something special or paying off an unexpected expense.

It's important to remember that these percentages won't work for everyone and that you can adjust them to suit your specific situation. For example, someone earning $40,000 a year may need to spend a higher percentage of their income on needs than someone earning $200,000 a year.

The pay-yourself-first budget

If you're someone who doesn't want to have set budget categories, you could try paying yourself first and letting everything else fall into place around that. To make this work, you need to know your rough fixed and chosen expenses each month and how much you have left over; to illustrate, let's say this is $1000. You'd then set up your finances so that you transfer $1000 into your savings account as soon as you get paid and leave everything else in your spending account for all your expenses during the month. This is a great method for prioritising your financial future and giving yourself flexibility to spend the rest of your money during the month.

A common challenge with this budget is that it's easy to be overly enthusiastic about how much we can transfer into our savings account, and then realise on day 25 of the month we've run out of money for groceries. If you have to dip into your savings at this point, it's worth reflecting on whether you paid yourself too much and need to reduce how much you transfer out at the beginning of each cycle, or if you would rather cut back on some of your discretionary spending. It's all about trial and error with this method!

The reverse budget

The reverse budget is based on the idea that if we give ourselves all our spending money for the month up front we'll very quickly find ways to spend it. This strategy flips things around and makes every day payday by dishing out only a small portion of spending money each day.

So, how does it work? First you'll need to know how much your fixed expenses are each month, how much you'd like to allow for your chosen expenses and how much you'll put aside for future-you. Then as soon as you're paid, move the money you've assigned to each category into separate accounts, and automate as many as your bills as possible to come out of your fixed-expenses account. Then it's time to automate a daily payment of the money set aside for chosen expenses into your spending account. For example, if you've got $1000 set aside each month for spending on things that add value to your life (your chosen expenses), you would transfer around $33 into your spending account each day.

Is it time to break up with your budget?

Budgets can come to a natural end when you're just not feeling it anymore. This might be because you find you're able to manage your money effectively with fewer or different rules, the method you started with just isn't working for you anymore or your life circumstances change. That's okay! A budget is just one tool you can use to manage your money. It shouldn't be making you miserable or taking control of your life. If it isn't useful, let it go.

The main thing that I want you to take away from this discussion is the importance of experimenting and creating a system that works for you. Your personal finances are personal, and what works for you might look completely different to what everyone else is doing. Money is a tool, and it's up to you how you choose to wield it.

Kicking financial goals

You've done a great job getting to this point. Thinking about debts, emergency funds, net worth and expenses can be hard and overwhelming, but please don't give up. Learning about money can be hard, but not learning will be harder. Take a break if you need, share what you're working on with a friend, but come back and keep going. It's time to get into something I love doing: setting money goals and creating a kick-arse plan for achieving them.

What are your goals? And do they involve money?

We all have different reasons for the choices we make in life, and some of the biggest and most important decisions we make involve money: where we work, where we live, what our goals are and how we spend our time. Many listeners of the podcast who previously thought that money was something that their future-selves could deal with changed their minds when they started to focus on a goals-led approach. There's probably something you'd absolutely love to do if you had the money, whether it's front of mind or brewing in the background. Take a European adventure, for example. Setting and then working towards that goal affects every part of your finances. You learn how to budget, save, spend meaningfully and even talk to loved ones about money, all through this one experience.

It works because it's meaningful to you. When you set a goal that matters to you and figure out a plan to reach it, you're suddenly buying into the idea that money can be used as a resource to improve your life. Being financially engaged is no longer something that's only for other people. You become a person who saves and works towards their goals (more on how this mindset works in chapter 3).

Working towards meaningful, specific goals also helps you to prioritise. Though many things are possible, you can't have everything at once. If saving for Europe is important to you, for example, you might need to suggest a home-cooked meal when your friend wants to go to a fancy restaurant, or delay buying a new phone until after you get back from your travels. When you know what your financial goals are, you can restructure your budget and spending to prioritise them.

Start with what you value

People tend to jump straight into things without getting to know their reasons why; however, understanding that 'why' can help them set goals that they actually care about. I don't want you working mindlessly towards a goal suggested by friends, family or society if it doesn't align with what you want out of your life. That's definitely not going to make you happy! If setting goals for yourself isn't something you've had much practice with, give yourself some grace. Turning off autopilot and looking inwards at what matters takes time, but figuring out what you value is a good place to start.

Though it's helpful at any stage in your personal finance journey, now is the time to identify what you value and the things that you want to spend your money on because they bring you joy. Some people are okay with spending lots of money on a new car. I'm not. I'd rather spend it on a trip to London and the theatre. You might prefer the free air and humidity of a beach in Spain. I'm not going to ask you to write out a list of values like you're at a corporate retreat; instead, you're going to look at this through the lens of spending money. I'll show you different ways you can use your money to boost your happiness in chapter 7, but first let's look at the value you're getting from your spending right now.

An activity I find useful for examining my priorities is writing a list of the ten things I spend the most money on (I typically look through the last three months' transactions) and another of the ten things that I enjoy spending on the most. I then compare these two lists to see how well they align.

✎ Your challenge now is to write your own two lists and then use them to figure out whether there are changes you want to make in the way you spend your money. (You can find a template for this activity at buyinghappiness.com.au.)

After making your lists, you might realise you're spending a lot on something you don't really care about (gourmet food, for example, if you're generally happy with a sandwich) and not much money on what really fulfils you (for example, hiking might make you feel amazing, but you hardly ever go). This is an example of a misalignment that can be addressed with some brainstorming and budget adjustment. You also might realise that some of the things you love doing the most don't actually cost that much money and can easily feature in your life more frequently.

Actively making changes to your budget to align your spending with what you value is the perfect place to start, but what about some bigger goals? That could look like buying your first home, taking a once-in-a-lifetime family holiday or being financially independent (more on that in chapter 10). Big goals need big plans, and they often require bigger changes than just cutting a few of those pesky subscriptions. So, how do you take a bigger goal and break it down into something that's actually achievable? Let's jump in!

Now let's set some goals

Okay, now you know where you're currently spending your money and you've started to figure out what you value, you're ready to set some goals that you're excited to achieve. One of the most important parts of setting goals is working backwards to make sure the goals are realistic (so you feel better once you reach them) and creating a plan to get there. I like to have just one short-term goal (achievable within 0–12 months), one medium-term goal (12 months–5 years) and one long-term money goal (5–10+ years) on the go at any one time, otherwise it starts getting messy and I stop making meaningful progress on any of them. Like everything in personal finance, however, your goals are unique to you and your circumstance, so you'll need to figure out what works for you. These are just the rough timeframes that work for me!

Let's start with tackling those short- and medium-term goals. Setting goals with shorter timeframes can be an easier way to start because you can control a lot of the variables. Let's take an $8000 overseas holiday to be taken next year as an example. Here's how I suggest approaching it. First, get as clear on the amount you need and the timeframe as possible. That'll give you your north star. Then break it down into the monthly milestones you'll have to hit to reach that goal. To save that $8000, for example, you'll need to put away just over $660 every month. I like to open a separate bank account for goals like this because that allows me to easily track my progress. Then it's time to take a look at your income and expenses, which you worked out earlier in this chapter, to see if there's even $660 available to be saved right now. If there is, great! You can set up an automatic payment of that amount into your holiday savings account each month until you hit your goal.

What if it would be tough to save $660 a month right now? That's completely normal! The way I see it, you've got some options. Often the goal amount and timeframe are negotiable, so consider whether you can make some changes in those areas to make your goal more achievable. You might also consider making some reductions to your spending to increase the amount left over to be saved at the end of each month. If you get any cash windfalls, such as a return at tax time, you can direct it straight to your goal. Taking on some extra shifts or gig economy work is another option to consider.

I like setting short- and medium-term goals because they can generally be broken down into concrete actions and tend to have clear end points, but sometimes our dreams are a bit bigger – and that's when it's time to think longer term. When it comes to big, audacious goals, such as financial independence, it's better to work backwards to figure out all the smaller milestones on the way. Since we'll be discussing financial independence in greater detail a little later in this book, here's an example of how that big goal can be broken down into detailed and actionable steps using this method of goal-setting:

> *I want to build an investment portfolio to support me financially, so I can cover my basic living costs without a day job. (What a dream, right?) If my expenses are roughly $40,000 a year, I estimate, at a minimum, I'll need $1,000,000 invested in a diversified portfolio. How do I achieve this without winning the lottery? I would need to invest approximately $1100 every month for 25 years, assuming an 8 per cent average yearly return over this time (not accounting for fees and taxes). As I can't currently invest $1100 every month, I'll need to make decisions to help increase my salary, lower my spending and find some other sources of income. I will automate as much of this plan as possible and check in on my goals regularly to see how I'm tracking.*

If you're setting investment goals, it's important to measure progress on the factors within your control, such as the amount you invest, rather than factors outside of your immediate control, like investment returns from one month to the next. As an investor, for example, you have no control over what the market does. Even if your plan is great, it's important that you give it time to work. It's easy to make the mistake of measuring long-term goals over short time frames and start losing motivation if the results aren't there right away. While it's important to check in regularly (monthly or quarterly) to see how you're progressing, you need to balance that with taking a longer-term view.

✎ It's time for action. Putting everything together, write out one short-, one medium- and one long-term money goal that you want to prioritise right now. Then come up with a rough plan on how you'll get there, plus some ideas to ensure your success. Your longer-term goal may involve investing, which we'll cover a little later in this book.

Don't worry – you don't need to have every detail figured out just yet! You can keep adding more detail to your plan as you progress.

Put your goals on autopilot

I find staying on top of my finances can be downright exhausting sometimes, and that's why I try to automate as much as possible – especially the things that will have a positive impact on my financial future, such as debt repayments, saving and investing. One of my investment automations has been running monthly for nearly seven years, with only one small interruption a few years ago. Every time I check in with the account balance, I'm reminded of the power that regularly saving or investing small bits of money has over time. Even better if it happens in the background without having to actively think about it!

Now you've set some goals, think about how you can automate the actions that will help you to reach them. This puts the money for your financial goals out of sight and mind (until you need it) and helps you stay consistent by removing the need to remember or decide at every stage of the process. For example, if you decide to save $250 each month, you can set up your bank account to automatically transfer that money into your savings account every time you get paid. That means you won't need to find time to sit down and make that payment manually – *and* you can't blow the money meant for your goals on discretionary items if it's not in your spending account to begin with!

Most banks offer the ability to set up automated transfers between your accounts, and some even let you split your pay cheque automatically according to your chosen percentages. Another helpful tool offered by some banks is an automatic round-up transfer. The idea is that the cost of every purchase is rounded up (usually to the nearest dollar, though some allow you to set the interval) and the difference is deposited into a nominated account. For example, if I buy a $4.50 coffee, 50c is automatically deposited into my travel savings account – and these small amounts all add up!

Finally, remember that not everything that can be automated is good for you. It's worth considering ways of adding friction to the things that take away from your financial future – Apple Pay, anyone? This includes things like monthly subscriptions (that you've stopped using but forgot to cancel) and big annual bills (where you might be able to shop around or negotiate a better rate).

✎ Your final step in this chapter is to go to your bank account and set up one automatic transfer that aligns with your money goals. (We'll explore how to automate your investments in chapter 8).

TL;DR

It might not seem like it, but building your financial confidence through the steps I've set out in these first two chapters will go a long way to setting you up for financial success. By knowing your numbers and working towards your goals, you'll free up time and resources to increase your overall life satisfaction and get on with the things that matter to you in life outside of your bank account.

- Money might solve your money problems, but it's important to focus on your own journey and avoid comparing your net worth to someone else's.
- Don't let your net worth determine your self-worth. A well-lived life is measured by much more than dollars and cents.
- Experiment to find a budgeting method that works for you, keeping in mind that a budget it just a tool that gives your money a job.
- Figure out what you spend your money on and what you love spending money on, and then see if you can find ways to align these things.
- Set yourself one short-, one medium- and one long-term goal, and then find ways to automate your progress towards them where possible.

3

Building your money mindset

Unpack your story, manage financial regrets and overcome limiting money beliefs

The mystery of human existence lies not in just staying alive, but in finding something to live for.
Fyodor Dostoevsky

If you were to win a million dollars today, what would you do with it? It's a fun hypothetical to ponder. It's easy to assume that the windfall would guarantee you financial success going forward, but US lottery winners are more likely to declare bankruptcy in the 3–5 years after their big win than the average American. Plus, they're not any happier in the long term. In fact, some research shows they might even enjoy regular activities, such as going for a walk or having a coffee, *less* after winning.

Financial results are more reliant on behaviour than IQ, connections or qualifications. This is why building a healthy money mindset is important. In this chapter, to help you to manage your finances better, you're going to get to know yourself better and ask, 'How is my current mindset serving me?' We'll start by exploring your money story and tackling limiting beliefs that might be holding you back, and then I'll share some suggestions for dealing with financial regrets. While this might seem straightforward, there are lots of important things to unpack in this chapter to make sure you're putting yourself in the best position to build a life you love.

What's your money story?

What do you remember about money when you were growing up? Did your parents give you money for the school canteen, buy you second-hand school uniforms or pay for dance lessons? Was money spoken about at home? Did you go grocery shopping together? Did you have a part time job? Did your parent tell you they couldn't afford to take you to the zoo? Did you go on family holidays overseas or did you spend the summer doing jobs around the home?

One of the reasons I love having conversations with people about their relationships with money (and I'll give you some pointers on this in chapter 5) is that I enjoy learning about how an individual's circumstances and experiences growing up thread into their tapestry today. Getting past my own curiosity, though, unpacking how your childhood and current environment influence your behaviour with money is important. For example, I grew up in a household that encouraged buying assets and meaningful experiences, and discouraged buying material items. This shaped my behaviour for a long time – and not necessarily in ways that aligned well with my own values. I'd even send some of my online purchases to a friend's address because I didn't want my parents' judgement, and it meant that I wasn't fully enjoying the purchases I made. Thankfully, I've found a happy medium and no longer feel ashamed about the ways I spend my money. I'm intentionally using it in ways that bring me happiness.

There are also links between childhood experiences and people's attitude to investing and ability to take risks – both of which are relevant to you on your personal finance journey. These core memories can resurface when setting money goals, investing, starting a business or planning for retirement, and they can influence your approach for better or for worse. The better you understand how you experienced money growing up, the better informed you'll be about your own values and tendencies when making financial decisions.

✎ Now it's time for you to reflect on your own money story. I want you to spend 30 minutes with a cup of coffee and a notepad, writing down everything that you remember about your experience with money when you were growing up.

Were there special things you remember getting or experiencing, or do you remember always missing out? Write about part-time jobs, purchases big and small, holidays, fights about money, after-school activities, your parents' careers and finance experiences, pocket money – basically, anything that comes to mind. You might rediscover some memories or feelings that you'd forgotten about. Also consider if you felt better or worse off than your classmates, friends and neighbours. Our feelings are often shaped by where we sat in comparison to those surrounding us.

Once you've let all these memories bubble to the surface, no matter how significant – or insignificant – they might seem, it's time to look at your story as a whole. Are there any insights or patterns that stand out to you? Could it be that your apprehensiveness to invest now is linked to a family member losing a sum of money early in your life? Maybe no-one around you saved or set goals. Was wealth idealised in your household or frowned upon? Can you see a pattern in the financial decisions you've made to date? Have a think about how your experiences might be shaping your current behaviour.

This is your money story. Understand it, but also know that you can change it. You're in the driver's seat for the next part of your journey.

You can change your story

Sometimes it makes sense to quit and walk away, but sometimes doing the hard thing is the right decision. It's difficult to know what the right decision is in the moment, and hindsight can be a tough teacher. However, I haven't had anyone tell me they regretted paying more attention to their financial future. Yes, it might be hard when you realise you've got a long way to go on your debt repayment journey, for example, but to paraphrase Glennon Doyle, you can do hard things.

I'm not going to be condescending. I won't say, 'If I can do it, so can you.' Our experiences are not the same. We all start our journeys at different points: some people have a 100m head start, while others can barely see the starting line. In your reflection earlier in this chapter, you might have uncovered some experiences or feelings that you don't want to repeat moving forwards. Noticing and acknowledging that is the first step. Then, keep taking small steps in a new direction, and don't feel you have to rush. If you've never saved or invested before, give yourself time to start becoming someone who does. It won't happen overnight, but you'll be surprised looking back in a year's time how much of a change you can make to your own story.

What's your 'why'?

Having excavated your past, it's time to focus on the future. One way you can get a better sense of what you want your money story to look like going forward is to understand why sorting out your finances is important to you. For me, building wealth is about choices. I want the option to focus on my career, spend more time with family or go on an extended adventure. So, I know my 'why', but what's yours? If you completed the activity in the previous chapter, you'll have a good idea of what you value spending money on. Now I want to add time into the mix, because there's a lot we can do with money in life, but we can't do it all at once. We have to prioritise.

✎ My friend Owen Rask suggests working through the following exercise to really get to the bottom of what you want in life. We don't often turn off autopilot and really think about the way we design our days. Plus, you might even realise in completing this exercise that there are some small changes you can make right away that'll have a meaningful impact on your happiness.

Take some time to answer each of these questions, noting it might take you a few weeks of coming back to the exercise to really figure it out. I'm going to show you how I worked through the exercise and include my responses as examples, but grab a pen and paper and do it yourself, too!

Think about all the things that you enjoy. (Make a list.)

I like:

- *running/walking*
- *deep conversations*
- *one-on-one time*
- *challenging myself*
- *learning and study*
- *books and reading*
- *group projects.*

And now think about the things you don't enjoy as much. (Make a list.)

I dislike:

- *crowded environments*
- *watching too much tv*
- *staying inside all day*
- *eating unhealthy food*
- *family/friend/work drama.*

With these lists at the front of your mind, I want you to think about how these things can be added and subtracted to design your ideal day. The more details you can add to really visualise this, the better!

✎ Now take this a step further by visualising your ideal work and leisure days. Once again, I'll share my own responses as examples for you.

What does your ideal Tuesday look like? (Describe it from wake up to bedtime. This is a workday.)

I'll start my day with a cup of tea I make at home using my teapot.

I'll then move my body by going for a walk or run.

I'll work on a meaningful project with other people, ideally in person.

I'll learn something new after work.

I'll prepare a healthy and tasty meal with a friend.

Then I'll tie off my perfect day by jumping back into a good book.

What does your ideal Saturday look like? (Describe it from wake up to bedtime. This is a day of leisure.)

I'll start my weekend off strong by going for a long run along the river.

I'll cook a big breakfast and eat it slowly since I'm not rushing out the door.

I'll go for a coffee walk with friends.

I'll spend some time learning something new or working on a creative project.

I'll have a good cup of tea with my family.

Then I'll do something fun like go to an improv comedy show or trivia with friends.

I'll tie off my perfect day by jumping into my freshly made bed and having a great sleep.

How far away are your current Tuesdays and Saturdays from your ideal days? Often our ideal days aren't that far apart from our current ones, and there might be some quick changes you can make to get better aligned. For example, if you want to wake up and go for a walk first thing, can you adjust your evening and morning routines to start prioritising this? If your current and ideal days very different, what major shifts do you need to make to get them closer? For example, if you want to spend more time with family and friends, what changes can you make to put that first in your schedule?

Now, building on this thinking, you're going to put together a vision board. Stay with me; I'm not talking about an aspirational collage with a picture of the beach, a pile of cash and the body you've always dreamed of. I'm talking about something much more practical, with a sprinkle of aspiration thrown in for good measure.

Using the following template, which you can download from buyinghappiness.com.au, use the descriptions and lists you've just made to align some of those likes and ideal days with your goals, by decade. You can do this with pen and paper, or using a digital tool like Google Docs or Notion, but ultimately you want to add as much detail about what you'd like to achieve, experience or buy as possible so you can visualise what you're working towards.

Table 1: Vision board template

20s	30s	40s	50s	60s and beyond

Brainstorm all those things you'd like to work towards, learn, achieve, experience or buy, and try to put them all into the template. Then add some more detail to what's coming up in the next decade to work out where it all might fit. If there's a money or time component, think through how that might fit in, too. Use all those fantastic goal-setting skills you learnt in the last chapter here! Then put this vision board somewhere you'll see it on a regular basis to remind you why working on your financial future matters, especially when you're feeling less motivated.

The point of this activity is to help you think bigger about how you can get the most value out of the only life you've got. It also pushes you to prioritise. For example, there are some things you can easily do in your 20s that might be a bit harder in your later years. Additionally, you might find that some life experiences on your list correspond to specific time periods in which it's ideal to spend more time and money on them. Consider, too, that you probably won't have the resources to do everything on your list this year – but you *can* work towards achieving those goals once you've articulated them.

This tool will be something you keep iterating over time, and will help bring everything you learn in this book together. Don't be afraid to get messy and keep changing things around until it feels like the puzzle pieces fit together!

Tackling limiting money beliefs

As you've worked through setting up your financial foundations, looked more closely at your money story and started to think about how you want to spend your time and money, you may have run up against some roadblocks already. This is normal. You're doing something new, challenging your past choices and thinking about what could be possible in your future, and your brain will be coming up a whole range of reasons why you can't do these things. These thoughts and stories that we tell ourselves, and that are actually keeping us from working towards the things we'd like to achieve, are called 'limiting beliefs'.

Hands up if any of these statements have ever run through your head before:

- I'm not smart enough.
- I'm not good with money.
- I don't have enough time.
- I'll never be wealthy.
- I don't deserve to have money.
- I'm afraid to make the wrong choice.

These are just some of the common limiting beliefs people have around money. Do any of these resonate with you? Though these thoughts are completely valid, they can limit your ability to take control of your financial future. The thing is, we all have unique backgrounds and a wide variety of experiences with money. If you do identify with one or more of these beliefs, I want you to start by asking whether this mindset is currently serving you. Has this thought pattern or story you've been telling yourself helped you on your money journey? Listeners have told me that many of these statements are reasons they haven't taken control of their own financial future, and the World Economic Forum found similar results globally when they asked people why they hadn't invested yet.

Though you mightn't be able to set aside these long-held beliefs immediately, education plays a big part in building your financial confidence over time. Acknowledging your current situation is the first step to improving it. So, let's go back to some of those common limiting money beliefs and think about some strategies to overcome them. I've included a few ideas, but get creative, do some research and have a think about what might work for you.

I'm not smart enough.

One of the biggest misconceptions about managing your money and investing well is that it has to be complicated. In reality, decent returns can be found using simple, no-frills ETFs to build a core portfolio (don't worry, I'll explain this later on). You don't need a PhD, some fancy finance qualification or even to be good with numbers to build a respectable long-term portfolio that sets you up financially, but everyone needs to have a basic understanding of what they are doing and manage their behaviour accordingly.

I'm not good with money.

Maybe you're not good with money *yet*. So, keep reading this book and schedule some time in your calendar to learn one thing about your finances each week. You can directly challenge this statement through taking action on a regular basis.

I don't have enough time.

Find 15 minutes a day or an hour a week in your calendar to work on your finances and stick to it. Committing this time now will pay off massively for future-you. Time is just how we allocate our priorities; there will always be too much to do, so break the task down and prioritise it.

I'll never be wealthy.

This is a common belief that stops people from ever taking the first step on their investing journey. Small amounts have a huge impact on your future if you give them time to grow. Many investors started where you are right now, so just take it one step at a time and think about your 'why'.

I'm afraid to make the wrong choice.

Not making a choice is still a choice. You don't need a perfect plan to start – you can learn as you go. Schedule in time to do the work, figure out your financial starting point and go from there. One step at a time!

Here are some other tips to consider:

- You can remove some elements of choice and decision fatigue by automating your saving and investing.

- Give yourself a deadline to avoid procrastination or overthinking.
- Remember that taking action is better than waiting for perfection.
- Consider the opportunity cost of waiting. For example, spending a year searching for the perfect broker means you're delaying the opportunity to benefit from compound interest.

✎ Your challenge now is to first identify one of your limiting money beliefs and then experiment with ideas for tackling that belief. You might need to try out a couple of strategies before you find a solution, but stick with it.

I'm now going to take you through two additional strategies that I think most readers of this book, and most people more generally, could benefit from. These directly tackle the limiting beliefs that stop you taking action.

Reframe your identity

Every action you take is a vote for the type of person you want to become.
James Clear

One strategy to overcome these limiting money beliefs that can cause havoc on our money journey is by reframing them, which can provide you with a new perspective. Instead of looking at the reasons why you *can't* save or invest, I want you to start thinking of yourself as someone who *can* manage their money, who *can* deal with their financial situation and who *is* an investor. As weird as it might sound, try saying this aloud:

> *I'm learning to manage my money well, I can manage the financial challenges life throws at me, I can save money for my goals and I can invest.*

It will take time to reframe your money identity, and it will need to be regularly reinforced through positive financial actions. It might sound like too much bother, but if you don't do it you'll always struggle with the mindset part of your finances. James Clear, author of the bestselling book *Atomic Habits*, suggests reframing your identity with statements like, 'I'm the type of person who…' By saying, 'I'm the type of person who saves money for upcoming purchases' instead of saying, 'I want to save money', you begin to integrate this statement into your identity.

If you've told yourself that you're 'bad with money' in the past, let's look at how you might be able to reframe this. Start by making small changes in the way you talk to yourself. You could, for example, say this:

> *I'm the type of person who is learning to manage my money well, so I can work towards reaching the savings goals I've set for myself.*

Then, instead of jumping straight to a big money goal and getting overwhelmed, set yourself small targets to work towards (and slowly increase) as you build your confidence around this new identity. Bit by bit you'll reinforce to yourself that you too can be someone who's on top of their finances, and you'll have the evidence to remind yourself. As James Clear says, every time you take a positive action, you're voting for your new identity.

✎ Now it's your turn. Is there an area of your finances, potentially one of the limiting money beliefs I've just run through, that could benefit from reframing? Consider starting with the way you're talking to yourself and finding actions you can start taking to back up your reframed money identity.

Get unstuck

It's easy to get stuck in the learning and planning zone, especially at the start of your journey. If you're reading this book, you're probably keen to take action, but the gap between learning and action can feel insurmountable. The thing is, when it comes to money, it's a practical skill rather than a theoretical one, so you need to start getting your hands dirty.

Something I like to remind myself of is that the perfect conditions for financial action don't exist. If we look closely, we'll always be able to find a reason to not pay off debt, save extra money or invest. When we realise there will never be a perfect time – or a perfect way – to do something, it takes a lot of pressure off our shoulders to make sure we have everything lined up before we make and execute a decision.

Yes, learning and making a plan is important – and analysis paralysis is real (more on that in the next chapter) – but don't get stuck there. Do you think you understand the gist of things and have a loose plan? It's time to get started. Nothing will change unless you do.

✎ Over to you now. Choose one task you've been thinking about for a while and take action today. You don't need the perfect conditions to make progress.

Dealing with financial regrets

When I speak to people getting started investing, one of the most common things I hear about is their regret that they didn't know about investing and compound interest a decade or two earlier and take action on that knowledge. It's tough to look at the numbers on a compound interest calculator and realise the difference ten or 20 years could have made, but don't beat yourself up about it. Instead, choose to focus on the knowledge and resources before you and maximise your time.

Regret can hold us back by making us feel like we've missed the boat and we'll never be able to make up for missed time – and that makes it difficult for us to reach our goals. With this in mind, I've come up with five ways to help you deal with and minimise regret on your personal finance journey.

Idea 1: Take action NOW

When I feel like I've missed the boat on something or get annoyed at my past self for not doing XYZ, I try to turn those feelings into action. I can't change past-Kate's decisions, but I most certainly *can* do something about present-Kate's. Turn those feelings into action today. Create a savings plan, go to the accountant and deal with your taxes, or finally take the time to sort out your retirement account. Whatever it is that you wish you'd figured out earlier, do it today. Start building the financial future that you want right now.

Idea 2: Reflect on the way you make decisions

If your goal is to minimise your regrets in life, it's essential to use this as a lens when making financial decisions. Projecting forward into the future, look back on the decision you're about to make. Use this vantage point to guide your decision-making and act accordingly.

It's also important to remember that many of your life decisions are not binary. If you make a financial choice now, you're not typically stuck with the results of that decision forever. Deciding to invest in a particular ETF or use a specific broker today doesn't mean you're not allowed to change your mind tomorrow. As you learn more about yourself and build your financial confidence, the decisions you make regarding your finances will change and evolve – and that's natural. Remember, you can change your mind.

Idea 3: Set yourself up for success

I'm a big fan of goal-setting and vision-boarding because these tools help us to get clear on our goals and priorities. If you haven't already, go back and complete the vision board earlier in this book, and then pick one short-term, one medium-term and one long-term goal to focus on. Doing this will help you to reduce your regrets in the long term. As an added bonus, when you look back, you'll have a record of what was important to you. It's not fair to mourn not achieving something that wasn't even a priority to you in the first place.

Idea 4: Acknowledge that sometimes you've just got to spend it

It's tricky to find equilibrium in life, and it's even more challenging when you're trying to balance spending, saving and investing your money. It forces you to make trade-offs; spend $100 today for an experience, or invest it and you could have over $200 in ten years. We might regret not hitting certain financial milestones, but we should also consider the inverse of that. Will you regret saying no to that family dinner or trip away with your friends? It's tough, but sometimes you've just got to spend the money.

Idea 5: Start talking about money

As they say, you don't know what you don't know. The more conversations you have with family, friends and colleagues, the more possibilities you'll become aware of. Plus, you never know what ripple effects these conversations might have. I won't sugar-coat it. It will be hard. But hard doesn't mean it's the wrong choice. We'll talk more about having money conversations in chapter 5.

TL;DR

Phew, this chapter was a big one! If you completed the activities, I just want you to pause and pat yourself on the back. This mindset work is important on your money journey and will make a big difference to the way you set and work towards financial goals in the long term. This all helps you to use your money and time better, prioritise what matters and start removing the barriers between you and your goals.

- Your money story matters. Spending time getting to know how you experienced money growing up and how it might be influencing you today will help you make better, more informed decisions.

- Having plenty of money is helpful, but it doesn't make a big difference to your happiness if you don't know how to spend it in a way that matters to you, so get to know your 'why'.
- Limiting money beliefs can get in the way of you making changes in your life and reaching your goals, but you can reframe them. Change the way you talk to yourself about money and back this up with small consistent actions.
- Don't let your regrets about past money decisions stop you from moving forward. Learn from them and start taking positive actions to change your financial future by making use of the resources you have available today.

4

Hack your brain

Overcome common behavioural traps, including the fear of making a mistake and analysis paralysis

The concept of 'enough' money doesn't necessarily mean you have no aspirations for more. It means you realize that if your expectations grow faster than your income you'll always be disappointed and taking too much risk.
Morgan Housel

Something peculiar happens when we start saving and investing: our brain starts playing tricks on us. Psychologists call these 'behavioural biases', and they can cause us to make irrational decisions with our money, get caught up in the next big thing and feel generally miserable, even if we have more money than we know what to do with.

Given we're all here to improve our relationship with money and sprinkle a little more happiness into our lives, it's important to address some common behavioural traps that can get in the way of our success. I'm also going to suggest some strategies you can use to overcome these biases (to hack your brain, if you will) and remain even-keeled and rational, even when it gets difficult. Although these traps are difficult to overcome entirely – we're only human, after all – this is another area of money where knowledge is power.

Fear of making a mistake

Have you ever lost money? I remember one school holidays I'd saved up $20 of pocket money. Naturally, the money was burning a hole in my pocket, and I was carrying it around with me, ready to spend it on the first thing that caught my eye (probably sweets). But then, tragedy struck. Somewhere in my travels the $20 made its way out of my pocket and into the wider world. I was devastated. The pain of losing that $20 was absolutely not proportionate to the happiness of receiving it.

My story, though overly dramatic when I recall it now, is analogous to something that many of us face every day as adults: the fear of losing money because we made a mistake and the pain that we'll feel as a result. The thing is, that fear vastly outweighs the happiness we feel making or being given the same amount of money.

Sure, it's good to have a healthy amount of fear about losing money. This is a book about using money to buy happiness, after all. But the problems start to occur when this fear holds you back from taking any action at all with your finances. Experts label this propensity to treat losses (even just the idea of them) as having more significance than gains as 'loss aversion'.

Consider this. Are you scared of losing money? Does loss feel personal to you? Has a fear of losing (or failing) stopped you from getting started in different areas of your life? These feelings can pop up in a number of ways. You might be ready to invest, for example, but your brain jumps in to stop you because you might lose money – and that's true. Investing involves risk. But it's also a proven way to build wealth over time and could play a big role in building the financial future you want (more on this in chapter 8). Avoiding feelings of fear and anxiety when it comes to money doesn't make those feelings go away. Instead, they build up over time, making it harder and harder to get started.

So how do you hack your brain if it's putting on the brakes? Here's what I'd suggest:

- **Spend some time learning.** The better you understand how money and investing works, the better you'll be able to stick to your plan when things feel uncertain.
- **Have a clear plan.** Write down your plan, including what you are investing in, how much and how often, your timeframe and your goals. You can then come back to this plan to remind yourself why what you're doing matters when you feel fear start to creep back in.
- **Start small.** You don't need to start with every dollar you have. Start small and build your confidence through action.
- **Invest regularly.** Along with starting small, build the habit and invest on a regular basis.
- **Think of what you've already achieved.** There's likely to be something in your life that you used to be scared of and that you now do without issue. Think about how you overcame that barrier and use the example as proof to yourself that you can persevere.
- **Be kind to yourself.** Money can feel overwhelming. Be kind to yourself during this journey; it'll take time to figure everything out and get comfortable being an investor.

Next time you feel like the fear of making a mistake is stopping you taking action, come back to this list and work through the suggestions. Although none of us wants to make mistakes, it's important to acknowledge that it's a natural part of the learning journey, and it's imperative we don't make the biggest mistake of all: never getting started.

Analysis paralysis

You're scrolling through Netflix, trying to figure out what show to watch. You've got some good recommendations to try, you can see what other viewers are enjoying and you can even watch some trailers, but an hour can disappear while you're trying to decide what to watch. This is analysis paralysis. While it's annoying when you're trying to have a movie night, analysis paralysis can be harmful for your wealth-building journey.

We have so many options these days, from bank accounts to investment opportunities, it can feel impossible to make a fully informed decision – even if we've read all the reviews, compared the fees and analysed the advantages and disadvantages. And more options don't make us happier. In fact, psychologist Barry Schwartz argues that a 'greater variety of choices actually makes us feel worse'. Then, if we do make a decision, we worry about whether we made the right choice. Schwartz calls these 'decision ghosts'. So given all the choices we have now, the natural desire to make the 'right' decision and the resulting drive to research, research, research, how do we combat analysis paralysis?

Analysis paralysis is a decision-making problem at its core, so let's tackle it that way. Choosing a brokerage account, which you'll need to buy shares (more on this in chapter 8), is a common challenge that people in my community experience analysis paralysis with. I'm going to take you through how I would suggest negotiating analysis paralysis with this specific challenge. I encourage you to take notes during your decision-making process, because it's a great way to learn from the decisions you make and reflect on why you made a certain choice down the track. Here's the process I suggest working through:

- First you need to identify the problem you're trying to solve and figure out where you're stuck. Start by writing down all the pieces of information you feel you need to know before you make a decision. Without doing this, you can get trapped in an endless research quest where you never feel ready to make a choice.

- Then use this list to do your research and write down what you discover. This information will form the foundational knowledge you need to make a decision further on in the process.
- Use this knowledge to generate options. Try to narrow down the choices of brokerage accounts to three suitable options that would fit your personal requirements. Any more than that will start to get overwhelming and reduce the chance that you'll make a decision.
- Now it's time to experiment. Give yourself a set time period to open an account with each of your top-three options and try them out. Make notes on what works and what doesn't, and assess how well each option meets your needs. Importantly, set yourself a due date to make a decision at the end of that trial period and move forward with your chosen brokerage account (remember this decision is not set in stone). Even better, find a friend to hold you accountable to this decision-making process.
- It's time to make a decision. Using all the information you've gathered and the experience you've had testing out each brokerage app, make a decision that is the closest fit to solving your problem. You don't need a perfect solution, but you do need to make a choice here.

Remember, not making a decision is still a decision. If you don't choose which brokerage account to open and use, for example, you're delaying your investing journey. And that's a choice. It might be the right choice for you, but the important thing is that you're conscious of this.

If you're struggling with analysis paralysis, it's also good to remind yourself that perfect doesn't exist in finance. Our lives are full of change, and searching for perfection can stop us from taking action. So, throw the word 'perfect' away and instead learn just enough to take your first small step. Each action you take builds your confidence, but waiting for the confidence to take action is futile.

✎ My challenge to you is to find one tiny action you can take today on a task you've been stuck in analysis paralysis mode with for a while.

Fear of missing out (FOMO)

If you've paid attention to the business news over the past decade you'll have seen countless stories of people both getting rich overnight and losing everything just as fast. GameStop, crypto and mysterious island festivals come to mind. But the thing is, this isn't a new phenomenon. Where there's money and incentive, greed and mania follow. It's easy to get caught up in groupthink when an opportunity or investment seems too good to miss out on. Plus, when it looks like everyone else is involved except you, the crowd can't be wrong … can it?

Unfortunately, when money is involved, the crowd (or the loudest person in the room) can lead you astray. The fear of missing out is a very human experience that can cause us to act irrationally and justify almost any decision without regard for the facts. Plus, FOMO has been shown to increase negative emotions such as envy, lower our self-esteem and generally makes us less satisfied with our lives, which is the opposite of what we're aiming for here.

Have you ever felt FOMO when it comes to your finances? Have you compared your finances to other people's? How has this affected your emotions and decision-making processes?

Here are some ways to combat FOMO, as someone wanting to build wealth and avoid the headaches that usually come your way if you follow the hype.

- Test your understanding. Can you explain to a friend in simple terms what the investment product or company does? This is a good test to see whether you've done any research or just picked up on a news story or tip from a taxi driver. If you can't, rethink whether it's a good investment for you.

- Write down your investing goals and your reasons for making each investment. Put this document somewhere you can access easily so you can refer to it in times of volatility, fear or FOMO.
- Remove your micro-investing and brokerage apps from your phone. This doesn't mean stop investing, but it'll stop you from making impulsive decisions to deviate from your plan without properly thinking through your actions.
- Reduce the noise you allow into your life. Don't let CNBC and Bloomberg headlines or push notifications alter your strategy without taking the time to properly do your research to work out if anything in your original investment plan has actually changed.
- Stay humble. It's easy to start overestimating your skills and knowledge once you're further into your investing journey, but that's when you start making mistakes. Keep your strategy simple, and don't try to outsmart the professionals.
- Work on ways to be happy on your own journey and not constantly compare your finances to your friends, family, colleagues or strangers on social media.

Mental accounting

A dollar always equals a dollar, right? Not so fast. There's a concept called 'mental accounting', which basically means there's a lot more to each dollar than meets the eye. Depending on where that dollar came from and where it's going, it can sometimes feel like 50 cents or $1.50. You might have experienced mental accounting without realising it. For example, have you ever received a gift card and found it much easier to spend than the money in your everyday account? I personally find it difficult to spend money on a massage, but it's a whole different thing if I receive a gift card or give a voucher to a friend. Weird how that works!

Assigning different significance to the various parts of our financial lives is a very human trait. We give money rules and assign it a value in our brain based on:

- where we got the money from (for example, a regular pay cheque, a tax refund or a gift)
- where the money is going (for example, life insurance, a trip overseas or repairing a broken tap)
- how we feel about a situation (for example, a planned repair versus an unexpected one)
- our personal values (what we value spending money on).

Imagine you just got a $1000 tax refund. If you're like some people, when you hear the news of a tax return coming your way you might have started daydreaming about all the ways you could spend that money: fancy sneakers, a weekend away, concert tickets… Many of the things you think of may be purchases you had no intention of making ten minutes earlier. That's mental accounting in action.

Mental accounting can cause us to spend illogically and more extravagantly because it alters our perception of the value of the money we receive and spend. Since our brains are wired this way, it's important to remind ourselves that we should be treating every dollar with significance, regardless of the where we got it from or where it's going. For example, if we had income from a side hustle on top of our day job, we should treat this money with the same importance, rather than viewing it as 'bonus money'.

Breaking free of mental accounting is all about spending money with intention. If you check in with your money goals when you receive an unexpected sum of money (for example, a tax return), you can make sure it's allocated in a way that makes current and future-you proud. Whether that's putting money into your retirement account or spending it on a holiday (maybe even both), don't let the trap of mental accounting warp your perception of the money you receive – or spend!

What is the next best step you can take with your money? Make a plan for unexpected income you receive, like tax refunds, bonuses and gifts. Don't let the money be spent on something that doesn't align with your goals and values. Plus, if you use it well, this money could help you supercharge the goals you set in chapter 2. Take a moment right now to jot down how you're allocating your imaginary money – even just on your phone. You never know, an unexpected windfall might happen sooner than you think!

Short-term thinking

Be aware of the natural inclination to fall into short-term thinking, even if you have solid long-term goals. Getting caught up in short-term returns and expecting our investments to perform overnight is a trap that's easy to fall into. Unfortunately, it can cause you to make decisions that won't serve you in the longer term and can lead you to make mistakes and lose money.

The key to avoiding short-term thinking is to remain focused on your long-term money goals. Here are a few ideas to help you do that:

- When you write your money goals down, make sure to consider the time frames for your short-, medium- and long-term goals, and do a common-sense check to see if they're realistic.
- Default to looking at the longest time frame available when looking at the past performance of an investment, not just the last 12 months.
- Understand how different types of investments have performed historically and the importance of taking a long-term view as an investor.
- Don't give too much weight to short-term news about a company or how the economy is performing.

A note on self-compassion

As a financial educator, I spend a lot of time talking to people about their futures and the decisions they make to set themselves up for success, but there's a huge amount of privilege in being able to make long-term career, financial and lifestyle decisions. To do this requires a decent amount of confidence that you will be able to meet your short-term needs. It's impossible to invest your money for ten years, for example, when you don't know if you'll have a roof over your head next month. Please be kind to yourself if this is you, and don't be discouraged if you can't think about your long-term financial goals yet. Instead, focus on the actions you can take to start adding a little bit of breathing room between your income and your expenses.

Shifting goalposts

Finally, let's explore how to prevent the feeling of never having enough from stopping us achieving our goals. There's a tendency for the scope of our goals to keep expanding as we reach each milestone. At the start of my money journey I was ecstatic to save my first $1000. Then, bit by bit, my expectations changed as I learnt more about money and investing and I started developing my goals. Aiming higher and higher is common, particularly at the beginning of our journey, but things can start to get complicated if there's no end point (or we keep letting it shift).

If you're not enough before money, you won't be enough with it. You need to find a way to be satisfied at some point, or you'll never be happy. Whether you've got $10,000, $100,000 or $1,000,000, it'll never be enough if you can't live an intentional life with the resources you have; your goalposts will just keep moving. The best way to get a handle on this is by getting really clear on your goal and why it matters. If you apply everything you've learnt so far in this book you should be able to set an actionable goal that means something to you and be able to articulate an end result that you can feel good about.

My goal is to become financially independent. You'll read more about the idea of financial independence in chapter 10, but the important thing to know right now is that it's a goal that really lends itself to shifting goalposts, not least because it can mean such different things to different people. Here are some of the questions I ask myself to combat this impulse:

- Have I had a really hard think about how much money would actually be enough to make me feel happy and financially secure? Can I articulate how I arrived at this number? If we don't fully define our goals, sometimes we work towards an arbitrary number that never feels like enough.
- How can I find ways to place a greater emphasis on the milestones along my journey and celebrate my progress as I go? This is important to stay motivated along the journey and not place all the pressure on the end result.
- Have I defined the end goal and why that's enough for me? What is my plan once I hit this goal? One of the reasons people shift their goalposts is that they feel don't have anything else to work towards once they've hit that milestone. So naturally, rather than face inertia, it seems sensible to move the goalposts.
- Have I thought about the 'what-ifs'? Another reason goals move is that once we reach them we worry about all the things that could go wrong, and it feels easier to just keep accumulating than to stop and examine these concerns.
- Have I considered what finance expert Ramit Sethi calls my 'rich life' is? That's the life where 'you look at your personal relationships, your finances and your ordinary days, and say, "Wow!"' This could prompt me to realise that I've already reached part of my goal, or I have some changes to make that aren't money-related.

As is the case when working towards financial independence, sometimes the goalposts aren't as clear as 'save $5000 for a holiday'. If you're working towards a bigger lifestyle goal, you'll have to figure out your own end point. No-one's going to tell you when you've got enough. Instead, you need to work out what that means to you by diving into your values and articulating the point at which you'll be satisfied with what you've achieved.

TL;DR

Money is tricky and can surface all sorts of interesting behaviours, so get curious! Question your decisions and investigate what your brain is telling you and why. Getting to understand these behavioural traps now will come in handy when you get to investing, as the more you know yourself and the way you act, the better you'll be able to combat all those ways your brain will try to lead you astray.

- Your brain will play tricks on you when you start saving and investing. Knowledge is power, so get to know yourself and your common behavioural biases better.
- By facing our worries about investing, we build the courage and confidence to keep going.
- Throw the word 'perfect' away and instead learn just enough to take your first small step.
- Default to looking at the longest timeframe available when looking at the past performance of an investment, not just the last 12 months.
- It's important to articulate your money goals, otherwise you might find that the goalposts keep moving and you never feel satisfied with the progress you've made and the wealth you've built.

5

Money talks

Have good conversations about money with people in your community

We have two ears and one mouth so that we can listen twice as much as we speak.
Epictetus

My friend's eyes slowly glazed over as I excitedly chattered on about saving for retirement. I was 18 years old and I hadn't yet realised quite how well society has trained us to tune out of money conversations and avoid them altogether. I also hadn't yet figured out just how emotional the topic of money can be and how different everyone's experiences are. As it turned out, my friend was a lot more interested in how she was going to pay her next phone bill than the merits of different retirement strategies. And rightly so. It was the wrong approach and the wrong time to bring it up. Too often it feels like someone is pushing an agenda, bringing a whole lot of judgement or palming off their own emotional baggage, and that's a big turn-off.

I'm still a huge fan of money conversations, but I'm a little more tactful these days. (There are still times I get ahead of myself, though.) Now I'm more aware that meeting people on their level is important, and that telling them the answer (although that's a grey area in itself) won't give them the tools they need to take control of their own financial future. We'll jump into some strategies for having these conversations later in this chapter. First we're going to have a real talk about why we *don't* talk about money and why that matters, discuss supportive ways to manage vulnerable conversations and open the can of worms that is money in relationships. This is going to feel like a lot, especially if talking about money isn't something you've ever done before, but it's worth it in so many ways.

Why don't we talk about money?

Many of us have been taught from an early age that we shouldn't talk about money, but I think that the taboo does much more harm than good. We're all thinking about money – every time we pay a bill, go to work or decide whether to take that holiday. And we're stressed about it, too. The American Psychological Association's *Stress in America 2022* study found that money, inflation and the economy are significant sources of stress for the majority of surveyed adults. The emotional strain of this is obvious, but the study also reports that stress is leading to all manner of health issues including headaches, tiredness, feeling overwhelmed and more physical complications. Even if we're not talking about money, it's affecting us much more than we realise. If the goal is to be happy, stress is going to make that difficult.

Talking openly about finances isn't the silver bullet for money-related stress, but it helps remove the culture of fear and shame. It helps us to know we're not alone, and we might even be able to find solutions to specific issues in the experiences of others. So many of us are struggling in similar ways – living pay cheque to pay cheque, using BNPL or racking up credit card debt – and yet it can feel like we're on our own. Coming from the other direction, if we have enough to get by or we're not struggling as much as others we know, it can also be easy to feel our problems aren't big enough to talk about, too. But that doesn't mean our financial stress isn't real.

It's become a lot more acceptable to talk about and get help for other issues we're going through, but money problems, such as being in debt, still seem to attract a lot of shame. This is borne out in the research, which finds feelings of shame go hand in hand with financial difficulties – and this can make our money problems worse. It can feel like we're supposed to get through them alone, but really it's a time when we need the support of our community. Talking about money might feel hard right now, but not talking about it will be harder in the long term. Start looking for the places where these conversations are happening, particularly if you're struggling.

As I mentioned in chapter 3, the more conversations you have with family, friends and colleagues, the more possibilities you'll become aware of, and you never know what ripple effects these discussions might have. For example, talking about switching to a low-fee superannuation provider might alert your friend that changing is something they're allowed to do rather than just sticking with the account their employer set up by default. Sometimes just having the conversations gives people the permission to do the same.

Good money conversations

If you've always wanted to bring up a money-related topic, but you just haven't known how to kick things off, this is for you. My suggestion is to start small. Don't jump straight into the deep end by talking about how much money you have in your investment accounts and what you get paid. If you do, chances are at least one person in the conversation is going to feel uncomfortable, possibly two by the time it's over, and I really want you to both have a positive experience. Instead, opt for something lighter and simpler. Everyone loves to talk about their savings goals, whether it's a new phone or a trip to Disneyland, and their best money-saving hacks. It's a fun and less intimidating introduction to those sticky money conversations and shows the other person that you're happy to have these discussions – without scaring them off. Of course, if they tell you they love investing and openly discuss their money goals with you, that's probably a good sign you can skip the small talk and jump straight into the big money conversations.

Getting vulnerable

Many of the more vulnerable conversations we desperately want to have require a great deal of trust between both parties. We can feel very judged and alone when it comes to our finances, especially if we're dealing with a challenging situation or feel like we've messed up. Showing that you're comfortable talking about financial topics, whether it's your go-to budget-friendly meal or your work on becoming debt-free, can help build trust over time with your community. If no-one in your friendship or family circles are talking about money, you can be the one to initiate them and say, 'Hey, it's safe to have these conversations with me.'

Hold up – vulnerable conversation alert! If someone opens up to you about their financial situation, keep in mind that you might be the first person they've shared these details with. Your response matters, and it could have a huge impact on your relationship moving forwards. Here are my suggestions in this scenario:

- Listen very carefully to what they say.
- Understand that their situation is unique to them and that their money story (which we touched on in chapter 3) will be different to yours.
- Don't compare their situation to your own (or your great-great-aunt's), unless they ask you for specific insights into those situations.
- Ask open-ended questions that will support conversation rather than closed questions that can be answered with a simple 'yes' or 'no'.

- Try to understand what they need from you in this moment. For example, if your friend shares that they've ended up with a huge credit card debt and feel lost, they might not be ready to hear how you think they should solve their problem. Asking if they'd like your help in any form right now or whether they just need a supportive ear is a good place to start.
- Be supportive, even if there's a small 'I told them this would happen' at the back of your mind. Showing even a hint of judgement can shut the whole conversation down.
- If they're looking for extra tools, you could share your favourite money resource (for example, a podcast or a book), and make a time to discuss it with them once they've consumed it.
- Remember, sometimes a professional will be much more effective at helping them solve their issue. Consider whether it's appropriate to suggest they seek help from a financial counsellor, psychologist, financial adviser, lawyer and so on, and ask whether they'd like a support person with them in the meeting.

Please don't let this list put you off being there for the hard conversations. It might be 30 minutes to you, but it could mean the world to the person opening up. You've got this!

Keeping an open mind

Remember, not everyone will learn, value or talk about money the way you do – and that's okay! It's worth keeping in mind that not everyone wants to have the same kind of conversations around money, and we all relate to it in different ways. None of us start our money journey from exactly the same point, and you just don't know if someone has had to work their way out of debt or if they've had a head start (unless they tell you, that is). Here are some key points to keep in mind:

- People want to learn about money in different ways.
- People relate to money in different ways.

- People talk about money in different ways.
- People do different things with their money.

You get my point. It might not make logical sense to you, but that's okay. We're all different, and we all have different values and priorities. These conversations work a lot better when they come from a place of compassion and curiosity than they do when we bring along judgement or assume the other person needs our advice.

Starting the conversation

You might be wondering how to start the conversation, because it can feel a bit awkward at the beginning. Here are some discussion prompts you can use to kickstart your money discussions. I've split them up into starter, intermediate and advanced categories. As you'll see, some prompts are designed to dig deeper than others, so these might be best used with closer friends and family with whom you've already spoken about money. Remember, there's a time and a place for money conversations, so use your judgement! It's important to meet your friends and family where they are in their journey, so choose conversation starters that suit. For example, if my friend is struggling to pay her rent this month, there may be some more practical ways that I can support her right now than jumping ahead to some of the more advanced prompts. Here are a few ideas to get you started.

Starter prompts:

- What is your favourite day of the week? If you had to pick from your list of favourite things to do on that day, how would you spend it?
- What's the one purchase that's added the most happiness to your life this year?
- What would you do if you won a million dollars?
- Tell me about one way you've saved money recently.
- What would you do right now if you didn't have to work?

Intermediate prompts:

- If I gave you $20,000 today, how would you spend, save or invest it?
- If you started a business, what would it be?
- What's your decision-making process for large purchases?
- What is the best piece of financial advice you've ever received?
- How did your parents approach money and financial conversations?

Advanced prompts:

- What does money mean to you?
- What would be enough for you (in the context of finances, career and achievements)?
- What is your biggest fear about money?
- How are you teaching/would you teach your children about money?
- What are your thoughts on intergenerational wealth and inheritances?

✎ Take one of these questions, answer it personally, and then challenge yourself to use the prompt to start a conversation with someone in your community this week.

When it doesn't go to plan

What if the conversation takes a turn or doesn't even happen? Don't be discouraged if your attempt to start a conversation about money misfires. It might not have been the right day or the right way to approach it with that particular person. For example, jumping in and talking about investing might be overwhelming for someone who's just trying to get themselves out of debt, but that doesn't mean you shouldn't try to talk about money ever again. Instead, learn from the experience and try a different approach next time. Remember to focus on meeting your friends and family where they are. While money can be a sensitive subject, one of the biggest mistakes we can make is to avoid the topic altogether.

Financially strong relationships

A lot of listeners of the show ask how to talk about money with a significant other. Their questions are big. How should we split expenses? Should we combine finances? What's the fairest way to approach our finances if one of us takes time off work to look after a child? How do I get my partner on board with our financial goals? These questions don't have clear-cut answers, unfortunately, because as we've established, every individual has a unique perspective on and relationship with money. When you bring two people together, things get even more challenging.

Getting on the same page

Considering that money is in the top five reasons couples fight (alongside sex, in-laws, alcohol or drug use and parenting), it's worth being proactive by thinking – and talking – about it. One study suggests that financial disagreements between couples are the strongest predictor of divorce and highlights that they can be challenging to resolve because our views on money are so bound up in our own history, values and goals (as we discussed in chapter 3).

So, how can couples approach this tricky topic as a team? When we really understand where another person is coming from in money discussions and what their priorities are, we start talking about money in the same language. This will seem like the most obvious advice, but communication and compromise are essential. A shared goal such as buying a property together, going on an overseas trip or starting a family can provide the impetus to create a budget and work towards that goal in ways that suit both people. Here are some pointers to support these conversations, keeping in mind that you should approach this in a way that works for your relationship and there might need to be a bit of trial and error:

1. **Set aside time.** In *The Barefoot Investor*, well-known Australian finance expert Scott Pape popularised the idea of having a money date night where you focus on each other and your shared financial future. Find a time when you're both in a space to have an honest and open-minded discussion about your finances together. This gives you time to prepare in advance and think about anything you want to share.
2. **Start with the big picture.** Rather than jumping straight into the numbers, spend time envisioning what you want your shared future to look like. Talking about your priorities in life and how you both want to use your money will help you to align how you spend your money and time together. (Jump back to the ideal day and vision board exercises in chapter 3 if you haven't completed them yet.) This is where you start to get on the same page, identify if you have conflicting goals and help your partner understand what's important to you (and vice versa). Remember: this part should be fun and exciting!
3. **Create a shared plan.** Now is the time to take all the dreams you have together and start turning them into reality using the goal-setting framework introduced in chapter 2. This includes prioritising your short-, medium- and long-term goals by working out what's most important to you both. You might realise at this point that you can't realistically achieve all your goals, so some of them might need to be modified or pushed back until a later date. This is also when you may need to start compromising, especially if you have conflicting goals, to find a shared path forward (more on that later). Just remember what you were told in school: keep your goals specific, measurable, achievable, relevant and time-bound.

4. **Start taking action.** Next, start working together to break down your goals into actionable steps to turn your dreams into reality. Get very clear on what actions you're each taking and when. While you're approaching these goals as a team, you don't need to have the same roles. One person could focus more on financial inputs, while the other spends more time researching and planning.
5. **Keep the conversation going.** Don't let your money talk dry up once you set your goals. It's important to keep the conversation going and support each other on your shared journey. Consider setting aside time every month to have a coffee and check in on your goals. This could expand to a wider financial conversation where you check in on your budget and spending, discuss your financial priorities for the month and keep each other accountable. It might feel challenging to talk about money at the start, but the more often you have these conversations, the easier it'll get.

As we'll explore in coming chapters, people have different risk tolerances and attitudes towards investing, which can cause complications. Reconciling these differences can take some discussion, but there is usually some compromise that can be reached to make both people feel comfortable. For example, a couple might decide that they want to invest together, but after working though the basics it may become apparent that one person is a lot less comfortable than the other with taking risks. Although they may have decided together that it makes sense to invest most of their shared money in a long-term diversified portfolio, actually doing so might leave one partner feeling very anxious because they don't like to see their money going up and down every day, which is part of investing.

So, what compromises could the couple consider to help them get comfortable with their financial goals? They could start with more discussions about money and how investing works, as the better they understand what they're investing in, the better they'll be able to emotionally manage the ups and downs. Another is to see a financial adviser together, so they can share their goals with an impartial third party with the expertise to suggest a strategy that suits both. They could also consider putting aside a larger cash buffer, such as 12 months of living expenses. Remember, just because the numbers make sense to do it one way, doesn't mean it's going to be the right strategy for every relationship.

A helpful resource here is the book *Eight Dates* by John and Julie Gottman, who have spent over 30 years studying relationships and communication. In a chapter dedicated to money and love they provide a great range of tools and prompts to understand your partner's money story and values.

✎ Spend some time (perhaps over a weekend) working out what you value individually, what you value as a couple and how you can build your financial goals together. It's worth returning to the exercises in chapter 3, which challenged you to design your ideal day and start putting some goals on a vision board, specifically looking for the areas of alignment that you can work towards as a couple. Where do you want similar things? Where do your ideal days and goals differ? Pull out the common threads and prioritise them in your shared vision. Then tackle the areas in which you want different things, focusing on communicating and finding ways you can both win together.

Negotiating conflicting goals

Sometimes partners' financial goals simply don't align. For example, you might want to invest so you're financially independent in ten years, but your partner is focused on living life in the moment and spending every dollar they earn. When couples' goals are misaligned like this, the resulting conflict can negatively affect not only financial outcomes but also motivation levels and confidence – not to mention it can make people feel less supported in their relationship. Research shows, however, that if we can find ways to positively manage the conflict between individual goals in a relationship, we're more likely to have positive results.

So, what can you do if your financial goal conflicts with your partner's? Here are some strategies to try:

- **Actively discuss why particular goals are important to you.** Your partner may not understand your goal and why you care so much about it. For example, if they are brand new to investing, it might be difficult for them to understand how it's possible for the two of you to become financially independent and why that's something you're working towards. Make sure to share your why, as well as the emotions, value and money history behind your goals.
- **Ask them what their goals are.** It's important to hear things from their perspective. What do they love spending their money and time on? What would they like to do with their money? What values (for example, freedom, independence and security) are most important to them? Remember, it's about both of you.
- **Find common ground and create a joint goal.** Consider how you can work together to create a shared goal that integrates both of your interests. Returning to that earlier example, is there a way to work towards financial independence while still enjoying regular trips together as a couple? Can you push your timeframe out to accommodate your partner's money values and take joint ownership of your shared financial goals? Approach these conversations by asking how you can both win, even if you can't both have everything you want at the same time.

It's essential during these conversations to actively listen to each other, because you've had a lot longer to understand your side of the story and why your goal is important to you than your partner has. You might need to take a break and revisit this conversation down the track or agree to work individually on your goals for a period of time.

A note on splitting bills

A common topic of conversation I have with friends, especially those in newer relationships, is how to approach shared expenses. Although what works will be different for everybody (and you'll probably choose a combination of approaches), here are three ways you can look at it:

- **Split everything equally.** Using this approach, every bill is split equally between the two of you. You might alternate paying for meals out, for instance, and you're probably keeping your finances separate. This is how most relationships start off in the beginning, and for some couples this is the perfect long-term approach.
- **Split costs proportionately to income.** This approach takes into account the differences in income for both individuals in the relationship. For example, if I earn $100,000 a year and my partner earns $50,000 a year, instead of splitting bills in half, I'd pay two-thirds. This allows both people in the relationship to make meaningful progress towards their financial goals.
- **Combine your finances.** Although this approach has been considered the norm for a long time, it's not the default option anymore. Some couples choose to combine some parts of their finances and keep other parts separate, such as individual accounts for discretionary spending, and that works for them. It's about figuring out what works for you and your shared goals. The important thing is that you're both transparent about your spending, savings and investment accounts.

The best way for you to manage your finances together will change over time, so it's worth revisiting this conversation yearly. Though I'm someone who values my independence, I'm mindful that splitting costs might not always be the right approach in a long-term relationship. For example, a couple's shared goals might involve one person taking time off work to study or start a business, or one member might have limited income for a time due to being a primary caregiver or experiencing illness. In these cases, it might be more appropriate to look at the total household income and how that can be used to support both people, rather than breaking each expense up. At the end of the day, come back to your shared values and goals and use plenty of communication to find a way forward that works for both of you.

Stay involved

It's worth acknowledging here that some people are perfectly happy to leave it up to their significant other to look after the money. The problem with this is that if the partner who deals with the finances can't be reached, becomes sick or passes away, financial responsibility will fall to that person anyway – and it can be very difficult for someone with little to no understanding of those finances to manage. This means that even if one member of a partnership doesn't want to be involved in making financial and investment decisions, it's still important that they have some idea of where the money is (and how to access it), know what goals they're working towards as a couple and gets updates on how they're progressing.

How to build a supportive community

We don't go on this journey in isolation. Friends, family and colleagues all play a role, so let's give them a good one. Here's what I'd suggest trying if you're keen to involve your community in your journey:

- **Share publicly.** This doesn't mean showing everyone your bank statements but rather sharing that you're trying to learn about your personal finances.
- **Get them involved.** People love to help, particularly when they hear you're passionate about what you're trying to achieve.

If you're trying to save money and want to spend time with your friends in a lower cost way, tell them about it.

- **Ask for help.** If someone if your community knows a lot about cooking on a budget or investing, for example, ask them to give you some pointers. Most people will be flattered to be asked, and you might just learn something awesome!

If you don't have anyone you can have these conversations with yet, or you're just not quite ready, consider these options:

- **Join an online community.** Even just observing the questions people ask might spark new ideas and questions.
- **Talk to an expert.** Think financial advisers, accountants and lawyers (more on talking to experts in a moment).
- **Connect through books, podcasts and online media.** I've included plenty of inspiration for this in the resource list at the end of this book.

Building a supportive community (whether that's in person or through other resources) plays a big role in helping you sort out your finances. Firstly, you're regularly reminded that you're not going through this alone, and you might be able to learn about people who have faced similar challenges to you. This community is also a way to keep you motivated; changing your financial future takes time and sometimes you'll need an extra push! Many long-term listeners of the podcast tell me they still listen each week, to remind themselves they're on the right track, make sure they're staying up to date with changes in the world of personal finance and for a regular nudge to keep taking actions that will buy them happiness now and in 20 years' time.

Once you start having money conversations, you might face some thoughts and feelings that you didn't expect, and it's easy to fall into the trap of comparison. For example, in having these conversations you might find out that someone you know earns three times what you do, received an inheritance or is in credit card debt, and it can be easy to start benchmarking yourself against them. But it's a trap. Don't let comparison steal your happiness. Your journey is your own. Use these conversations instead to learn, to gain a greater understanding about how your friends and family think.

Be wary, too, of becoming so focused on money that you discuss the cost of things and investment ideas at every opportunity. This can be exhausting for everyone involved, so it's important to find a healthy balance. If people think you're becoming obsessed with money, it might be an indicator that you need to dial down the money talk, and focus a little less on the numbers and more on life outside the spreadsheet. You might need to mute a money group or account, consume content in a different space or speak to a professional, such as a counsellor, if you find you're getting sucked down a money rabbit hole.

A note on borrowing from and lending money to family and friends

Chances are you've lent money to a friend or family member before. I've personally benefited from borrowing money from a family member when I left home at 17 to join the Air Force. It's natural to want to help our friends and family, and according to a recent survey, 60 per cent of adults in the USA have given money to friends or family with the expectation of being paid back. Unfortunately, however, more than a third of adults who've lent money have been negatively impacted by doing so, be that by the money not being paid back or the resulting damage to the relationship.

The way we lend and pay back money is a reflection of character. If you lend money to someone, you have to be prepared that it won't make its way back to you, and at some point you might have to decide between the money or the relationship. It's worth considering this the next time you borrow or lend money to family or friends, because money doesn't exist in a vacuum: the impact of the decisions you make in this area can ripple more widely than you might expect.

Engaging a professional

Never forget that no-one is going to care as much about your money and financial future as you will. At the end of the day, your money is your responsibility. Don't get me wrong; I'm a big fan of bringing in the right professionals to help you along your journey – experts such as financial advisers, accountants and lawyers – but you need to stay engaged throughout the process. Though you won't know everything about their area of expertise (that's why you're working with them), it's important that you know enough to common-sense check what they're saying and ensure they're appropriately qualified to help you.

Here are some questions to consider asking any professional you're thinking of involving with your finances:

- **What are your experiences and qualifications in your area of expertise?** This will differ based on the type of professional, but make sure they're qualified and registered to provide you with advice (where applicable).
- **Have you helped clients in similar situations to me?** Many professionals focus on helping a particular type of person or solving specific problems, so ask questions to make sure they can understand and specifically help in your situation.
- **Are you happy to answer questions in person or via email?** I suggest that you try asking them a question and see how they respond to you. You're looking for someone that doesn't talk down to you, who listens to what you say and explains everything clearly to you in a way you understand.
- **Am I able to speak to any of your previous clients or read some verified testimonials?** This may provide you with further guidance on whether they're a good fit for you.
- **Can you provide me with a clear and transparent list of costs in writing?** A good professional should be able to account for their fees and provide you a rough estimate of the cost at the

start so you can make an informed decision about whether to engage them.

- **Are you affiliated with or receiving commissions from any other businesses?** While this isn't a red flag in itself (it's the way some parts of the finance industry are run), it's important that you understand if there are any conflicts of interest and how they are managed. You also want to make sure they are providing you with the best possible advice for your specific situation, without the influence of any other incentives.

Make sure you feel comfortable working with this person or company, but don't abdicate all your power. Get curious and ask questions throughout the process. It's your money, after all.

TL;DR

Money conversations are important, and they can have a large impact on your overall happiness levels. It can be difficult if you can't share the highs and lows of your financial journey with those closest to you, especially when you need their support and encouragement along the way. I can't promise it'll be easy at the start, but every money conversation you have helps you gain greater understanding and awareness of your own and others' situations.

- When it comes to having money conversations, meet your friends and family where they are, not where you want them to be.
- Be careful not to jump into problem-solving mode. Sometimes people just need to vent or need to figure out the solution on their own. Start listening and ask how you can best support them in that moment.
- Don't be discouraged if your attempt to start a conversation about money misfires. It might not be the right day or the right way to approach it with that person.

- Financial disagreements are a big reason relationships end, so start proactively talking about money and finding ways to align your financial goals.
- As you build your money community with family and friends and add other resources, you'll find support, motivation and accountability. These are all essential tools on your journey.
- Use experts like financial advisers and accountants on your journey, but don't give away your power. Remember to ask questions and make sure you understand the plan.

6

Spend your time better

Enjoy the present while investing in the future

You can have it all. Just not all at once.
Oprah Winfrey

We spend so much of our lives just waiting for time to pass – willing the workday to be over, watching the microwave count down to zero, wishing that the months between us and our holiday plans would pass in an instant. We're always looking to the next moment, when things will be better. But when we do this, we're slowly, unthinkingly, spending our most precious commodity: time.

Research shows that the more in control of our time, and consequently our lives, we feel, the happier we are. Though we all have the same 24 hours in a day, how each of us experiences that time depends on our circumstances, responsibilities and values. This chapter is all about helping you to make the most of the time you do have to make yourself happy – both now and in the future. To do that, I'm going to show you how time and money – and also happiness – are connected and explore ways you can maintain balance between these elements when working towards big financial goals. I'll also dive into using time more intentionally, rethinking the typical approach to work and managing distractions.

Time and your personal finance journey

We talk about time and money in very similar ways. We choose how we *spend* our time, we look for ways to *save* ourselves time and we *invest* time in things like relationships. If someone gave you $8760 in cash right now, it's likely you'd spend a little bit of time thinking about how to spend it, right? But do you spend much time thinking about how you're going use the 8760 hours you're given every year? Consider too that if you were to spend the money, you could always earn more, while the time would be gone for good.

Your time is an asset that can be converted into money, achievements, better relationships and more choices, depending on how you spend it. If you invest all your time in exchange for money right now, you might end up burnt out and miserable. On the other hand, if you spend all your time maximising the enjoyment you can get right now, you might look back in ten years wishing you'd invested a little more time in your career, health and financial future. Add into the mix the idea that you can also use your time today to create wealth and get more choice over how you spend your days in the future (we'll jump into that more in chapter 10) and things start to feel even more complicated. Thankfully, you don't have to pick one of these options or strategies and then live with your choice forever. You can enjoy life, reach your goals *and* invest in your future; it's just a matter of prioritisation and balance.

Balancing present and future time

You can afford to spend your time on anything, but not everything, so it's essential to choose wisely. This is one of the challenges Derek Sivers considers in *Hell Yeah or No: What's Worth Doing*. According to Sivers, a 'present-focus' is necessary to enjoy life. However, 'too much present-focus can prevent the deeper happiness of achievement'.

Enter, delayed gratification: the act of resisting an immediate reward (for example, spending time and money on an immediate happiness boost) with the hope that the long-term reward (for example, buying a first home) will be better. Though it can be difficult, getting comfortable with delayed gratification is a particularly important skill for working towards big goals, and it can have powerful results over a lifetime. (More on those results in chapter 8). Much like too much present-focus, however, an overcorrection towards delayed gratification can negatively affect our happiness in the meantime.

Let's take saving up to purchase a first home as an example. If someone is starting from scratch, this goal could take quite a few years to achieve and require serious attention on how much they're saving each month. Reaching this goal is likely to fill them with a sense of accomplishment and add to their happiness levels. The problem is if in the single-minded pursuit of their goal they focus solely on making and saving money, saying yes to extra work and no to spending time with friends for years, they might find they miss a huge amount of life in the process.

We get a lot of happiness from working towards long-term goals, but sometimes it stops us being happy right now. In the field of positive psychology, Dr Martin Seligman's PERMA model presents positive emotion, engagement, relationships, meaning and accomplishment as the building blocks of a happy life. Pursuing just one of these, like accomplishment, at the exclusion of all the others isn't a recipe for success.

So, what's the solution? How do you work towards your big goals while remaining present and enjoying life? It comes down to balance and priorities. Finding lower-cost ways to engage in meaningful relationships, pushing your goals back by a year or two for important experiences in the shorter term and checking in on your goals (and actions) regularly to make sure they're not making you miserable are just a few ideas to work on that balance.

You could also look at your life as being made up of seasons. The idea is that in one period of time you can mainly focus on reaching a specific goal, spending your time accordingly. Then you might step back and use your time in a more balanced way in a subsequent season. It's also worth noting that there are certain times in life where it is more opportune for you to do particular things than other times. For example, hiking the Pacific Crest Trail in the USA might be something you have the time and energy to do in your 20s, but not in your 50s. Conversely, a cruise in Antarctica might be something you leave until you have the financial resources in your 60s.

Think about all those life experiences you have on your bucket list and consider if you can prioritise them into different life stages. (You could use the vision board exercise from chapter 3 as a framework.) This isn't about prioritising your finances at the expense of your experience goals. Rather, it's about being strategic about the way you allocate your time and resources. It might be the reality check you need to go, 'Hey, I actually might not have the opportunity to live abroad once I start a family, which I also plan to do. I should focus on moving overseas in the next few years.' Life is full of uncertainty, and there's always the possibility that it'll be a lot longer or shorter than expected. Organising the life experiences you want to have according to different parts of life is one strategy to manage your competing priorities and finite resources.

The 'I'll be happy when...' trap

Bestselling author of *Four Thousand Weeks*, a book about the finitude of time in life, Oliver Burkeman describes life as 'a succession of present moments' where you'll 'probably never get to the point where you feel you have things in perfect working order'. This is a call to arms to remind us that if we keep postponing our enjoyment of life into the future we're wasting the moments of our lives right now.

This is something I can struggle with. I've always loved setting goals, but without me even noticing, it became a habit to always be working towards something. For example, I couldn't just start running; I had to work towards a half marathon. I fell into the 'I'll be happy when…' trap, postponing my enjoyment of my day-to-day until I met some arbitrary goal.

Does that sound familiar? You can break out of this mindset by reducing the number of goals you set yourself, and clearly identify the weekly time commitment, achievement timeframe and completion criteria. The key is to break down your big, lofty goal into meaningful steps so you can enjoy and celebrate the journey, rather than quarantining those feelings of happiness and accomplishment on the other side of the finish line.

All you have is this moment right now, so you need to find small ways to pull yourself out of the future and into the present. This might be writing down or telling someone what you're grateful for today, just taking the time to be still or celebrating your progress so far. It took time, but I'm slowly getting to the point where I can enjoy running by itself, not just because I'm getting faster or working towards a new milestone. I've changed my definition of satisfaction and success to incorporate the process. After all, that's where I spend 99 per cent of my time.

When setting goals – and sticking to them – is difficult

Many people have the opposite problem, but it mightn't be a simple case of disinterest in the principles of delayed gratification. Hal Hershfield suggests in his book *Your Future Self* that 'to make better decisions today that create happier tomorrows, we need to find ways to close the gap between our current and future selves'. However, research suggests that some people find it challenging to think about and allocate resources to their future selves because they feel so disconnected from the very idea.

In one study on improving this connection between the present and future self, participants who were given realistically aged photos of themselves indicated an increased likelihood that they would save and invest for their future. If you're someone who doesn't usually like to set goals and has difficulty feeling connected to your future self, you could try this using a website that ages up a current photo of yourself by 30+ years.

Hershfield also suggests that we rely 'too much on our present self's feelings and circumstances' and that we can project them 'onto a future self who might not feel the same way'. Although we might not feel like spending our time studying on the weekend, helping a friend move house or investing for our retirement right now, that doesn't mean we'll feel the same way in the future. I challenge you to spend some time visualising your future self – with or without the assistance of technology – and consider if there are any changes you want to make to how you spend your time now that will help your future self.

Spending time intentionally

Given these discussions about balancing present and future time, and not falling into the 'I'll be happy when…' trap, how can you start spending your time more intentionally right now to maximise the value you get from your days? I mentioned in chapter 2 that it's possible to adjust your spending to prioritise the areas that bring you the most happiness (and I'll cover it in even more detail in the next chapter), but now I'm going to show you how to do that with your time.

Do you often find yourself saying that you're busy? It's common. Our society treats being busy as a badge of honour. It celebrates 'the hustle', massive to-do lists and jam-packed calendars. But in buying into this, we tend to neglect the small moments: opening up a good book and reading for hours, having long conversations with friends or wandering directionless in nature.

✎ Reflect on the times in the past seven days when you've used the word 'busy' to answer someone's question or as a reason for not doing what excites you or makes you happy. Is this something you might like to challenge or change in your life?

Audit your life

By being more aware of how you spend your time now, you can be more intentional about and have more control over how you spend it in the future, which studies show adds to our overall sense of wellbeing. In a similar vein, mindset coach Sarah Scully-Leaf spoke on the podcast about the importance of getting clear on where time and energy is being spent, and suggested looking at ten key areas:

1. health
2. self
3. family
4. friends
5. intimate relationships
6. work
7. finances
8. adventure
9. hobbies
10. purpose.

Most of us have a general sense of how we use our time, but we don't always break it down or think about it as deeply as we did our finances in the earlier chapters of this book. Let's change that now by using these ten key areas as a framework for completing a life audit.

First give yourself a score out of ten for the priority you currently allocate to each of these ten key areas, and then write down why you gave yourself each score. For example, I might score myself 1/10 in 'Hobbies' because I've completely neglected them for the past year due to the demands of my job.

The next step is to write down scores you'd like to reach in each area in the next 12 months. This will be based on how important each of these ten areas are at this stage in your life and how much time you want to spend on them. This should be realistic. For example, you're probably going to need to allocate time to work (but perhaps you could decrease the hours or mental energy involved; more on this in a moment), and though writing down 10/10 next to all ten areas might feel good, in practice not everything can take top priority because you only have a finite supply of time.

Then write down why you want to work towards each ideal score and how you plan to do that. For example, I'd love to spend more time on my favourite hobbies, such as surfing, and increase my score in this area to 6/10 because I know that will make me happier.

Finally, go through each of the ten areas, consider the difference between your current and target scores and strategise how you can close the gaps. You don't need to make huge changes overnight; instead, try to identify some small actions you can begin taking now to bring them into alignment.

This exercise is designed to help you find out where you spend your time currently and where you'd ideally like to spend it. It's important to give this a reality check, as there's a time for everything, but not all at once. This is an activity you can come back to every year, because as we go through life, our priorities, values and goals keep evolving, and that's a good thing! Let the way you spend your time evolve as well.

Trading money for time

If you find it difficult to prioritise the things that make you happy because you don't have enough time, you might need to make some bigger changes. One option you can explore is exchanging your money for more time. Consider this: is time or money more important to you? One of the best conversations I've ever had on the podcast was with Nir Eyal, best-selling author of *Indistractable*. In Eyal's opinion, time is much more important than money. Why? Because you can always get more money, but you can never get more time. It's not about being 'productive' every minute of the day but living life with more intention than we typically do.

Ashley Whillans of Harvard Business School has spent years researching the trade-offs between time and money in our lives.

In exploring the question 'Give up money to have more time or give up time to have more money?' she found that individuals who prioritised having more time over having more money generally had greater levels of happiness. Whillans then took her research a step further to see the impact of using money to delegate less favourable (and time consuming) tasks such as cleaning the house or doing taxes. I doubt you'll be surprised that she found that outsourcing some of these tasks added to participants' overall life satisfaction.

I've recently exchanged money for more time myself. Moving house is a messy process (in more than one sense of the word), and there's a lot of stuff to get done. Despite the fact it was already costing an arm and a leg, I decided to pay for a full house and carpet steam clean. This was a trade-off between the money I paid for the service, which I could've used to invest, and my time, knowing I was already time-poor and cleaning the house to the standard of paid professionals would've taken much more time than I was willing to spend. I made the choice to reduce my stress, increase my time and make the experience more pleasant.

✎ Now I want you to consider some tasks you have that you don't enjoy, that take up a lot of time or both. Write down the time they take and the way they make you feel after completing them. Then brainstorm a list of small solutions you could put in place and their approximate costs. Pick one of these solutions and give it a shot to see whether it improves your week. Here are some examples:

- Paying for a cleaner to free up 5–10 hours a week that you're able to spend with family and clears some of your mental load, knowing the house will always be relatively tidy when you have friends over.
- Buying a fruit and vegetable box that's delivered to your home from your local grocers means you don't have to spend ages figuring out what to buy, get inspired to cook new dishes and know you've got healthy snacks at home.

- Hiring a local student to mow your lawn to avoid purchasing, storing and paying for the ongoing upkeep of a lawnmower – plus spending the time it would actually take to mow the lawn.

There's a trap in this trade-off, though, and maybe we shouldn't delegate every annoying or time-consuming task. Burkeman argues that while convenience might make our life objectively easier, it doesn't necessarily mean that 'easiness is truly what's most valuable in any given context'. We sometimes forget while trying to make our lives as efficient as possible that some of the most meaningful parts come from the discomfort and inconvenience. Whillans's research also suggests there's a point at which outsourcing tasks starts to undermine our pursuit of happiness.

For example, though writing a Christmas or birthday card might take much more time than sending a quick text, the card probably carries greater meaning. I could pay for my food to be delivered, or I could allocate time to walk to my local food stores and connect with the staff and customers there. While he could easily pay for a handmade loaf of bread, one of my friends gains significant pleasure from the long (and in my opinion arduous) process of making his own. Remember that a perfectly smooth life shouldn't be the goal. By allowing bumps in the road, you might just surprise yourself with new experiences, friendships and a better understanding of yourself. It's up to you to intentionally choose which bits to smooth over and which bits to leave the jagged edges on – and that'll require experimentation.

Showing up

Studies show that personal relationships are extremely important to overall happiness levels, and this is why it's worth discussing the importance of showing up. This is another way we can use our time intentionally, not only to support loved ones, but also to strengthen personal relationships – the biggest contributor to happiness over our lifetimes.

There are pivotal moments in life where we have to show up. This isn't just about those big moments like weddings, funerals and birthdays. It's also about the tough times when a close friend's mum passes away, they get a tough diagnosis or they have a pregnancy loss. We need to be there for the good times and bad times in the lives of our loved ones, because these things are felt deeply for many years to come. The emergency fund that we discussed in chapter 1 can buy us the capacity to show up in these important moments. There's a huge privilege in being able to do this, but anecdotally, it's worth every cent. This all goes to illustrate the importance of having more control over your time and being aware of what you say yes and no to. Before you tell your friends and family that you're too busy to come over because of work, study or better plans, just remember that your actions within your relationships compound over time.

Given how precious your time is, don't discount how powerful it is to give it away – both to those you love and to causes that you care about. This could look like volunteering with an organisation that's important to you, offering to cook some meals for a friend who's having a tough time or helping a sibling move house. Even better, research shows that the more time people give away, the more time affluent they feel (more on time affluence in a moment). Simply put, the more you give, the more you get. Plus, the same study also found that 'people who give time feel more capable, confident, and useful' – bonus!

✎ Try this now. Find 30 minutes in your schedule this week and give it away freely to someone else. See if they'd like a hand with something, take them a coffee or just give them a call.

A note on regrets

I explored how regret – and the fear of regret – can get in the way of taking action with money in chapter 3, but I'm returning to it here because it also ties into the way we spend and invest our time. One of the ways we can incorporate intentionality into how we use our time right now is to imagine what regrets we might have in the future if we don't change the way we're spending our days. Regret is an interesting feeling, and it's one that people tend to be uncomfortable sitting with for long. Maybe you regret not starting to invest sooner, wish you'd travelled when you had the chance or spent more time with your parents after leaving home.

In *The Top Five Regrets of the Dying*, palliative care nurse Bronnie Ware shares five statements that pop up again and again in conversations with patients at the end of their lives:

1. I wish I'd had the courage to live a life true to myself, not the life others expected of me.
2. I wish I hadn't worked so hard.
3. I wish I'd had the courage to express my feelings.
4. I wish I'd stayed in touch with my friends.
5. I wish I'd let myself be happier.

Do any of these stand out to you? Imagining how you might feel at the end of your life, what changes could you make today to reduce the likelihood of having these regrets?

I want to give you something else to consider now, especially if you already have regrets. What if you don't look at regret as a negative feeling, as something to be avoided at all costs? What if, instead, you could use it as a tool to learn from, to better understand the choices you've made and how you've changed over time? What if you could look at your regrets as proof that you're not the same person you were in the past? As Daniel Pink, author of *The Power of Regret*, writes, 'Regret makes me human. Regret makes me better. Regret makes me hope.' I take this to mean that regret doesn't have to be a source of pain. Rather, it shows me that my priorities and values have changed and the way I use my time today is different to how I used to use it. You need to keep in mind that the person who you used to be, is not the person you are now, or the person you are starting to become.

We make a huge number of decisions every day (some estimate the number to be 35,000), and there's no way we can get them all right all the time. By reading this book you're choosing to invest in your future; you're learning and growing. As a result, I'm sure you'll regret some of today's choices in a decade's time, but I'd argue that's good – it means you're growing.

Time and work

Coming back to the idea of using time with intention, a big contributor to our happiness is time affluence. The Merriam-Webster Dictionary defines 'affluence' as 'an abundant flow or supply', and in the context of time, it flips the feelings that many of us have. Does the phrase 'I just don't have the time' feel familiar to you? If you're constantly feeling time-poor, like you never have enough hours in the day to work, exercise, spend time with family, keep on top of life admin and have new experiences, it might be worth considering changing the way you work to gain back a feeling of time affluence.

Maybe you truly love what you do, but could dropping down to four days a week, working overseas or jumping into a different industry change your experience for the better? Here are some starter questions to help you reflect on this:

- What are the elements of my current job that I do and don't enjoy?
- If I don't enjoy my job, is it the workplace and culture, or is it the role itself?
- What kind of team or environment do I enjoy working in?
- How much happier would I be if I dropped back to three or four days a week?
- Could I do my current job overseas?
- If I want to change careers, what skills and qualifications will I need?
- Could I do my job as a freelancer, contractor or casual?

Though you'll likely need to allocate some of your time to work, it's important that it isn't making you miserable. Think about whether there are any changes you can make to the way you work that could make you feel a little more time affluent.

Consider mini retirements

What if you could experience extended – and concentrated – periods of time affluence? Enter, mini retirements. There's no set definition, but it could look something like taking 3–6 months off every five years to work on a personal project, go on an adventure, start a new course, spend more time with family and friends or just catch up on your growing pile of unread books (it can't be just me with that problem).

In *The Happiness of Pursuit*, Chris Guillebeau talks about the purpose of a quest, that can bring additional 'meaning and fulfillment to our lives'. Guillebeau goes on to say that 'a quest has a few key features, including a clear goal, a real challenge, and a set of milestones along the way'. This could be anything from road tripping around Europe to learning a new language or growing a vegetable garden from scratch. We have so many choices now with the way we live, and it's up to us to get creative about how we use our time.

Why wait until you're over 60, when you could design your finances, career and life around regular periods of time off now? This won't work for everyone, but it could be an interesting way to balance enjoying your time and money now.

Managing distraction to make the most of your time

Distractions stop you from achieving your goals. Essentially, they're actions that move you away from the things that you want – and they're everywhere. They seem to suck up time at every turn. Podcasts, social media, streaming services and a constant barrage of notifications are all competing for your attention.

Distractions will always exist; managing them is your responsibility. So, what's the plan? In this section I'm going to walk through a few strategies for making the most of your time right now. Here are a few strategies to start with:

- **Avoid an endless to-do list.** Instead, rank the tasks you need to do by priority, try estimating how much time each task will take and put each task into your calendar (blocking out the required amount of time).
- **Find an accountability buddy.** Find someone who can keep you accountable for how you spend your time. For example, if you want to spend three hours distraction-free and working on a creative project every weekend, find a friend who will hold you to your intentions.
- **Remove distractions from your environment.** If you want to spend focused time working on your goals, find ways to remove distractions such as people, technology and noise from your environment.

Before I discuss scheduling time to waste and give you some suggestions for improving your digital life, I want to pause and think a little deeper about what's really behind distraction. We love to blame technology and other people for our lack of focus, but they're purely a proxy expression of distraction, and not the root cause. On the podcast, Eyal shared that 90 per cent of our distractions are triggered by an internal feeling of discomfort that we don't know how to deal with and would prefer to be distracted from. If we don't spend time getting to the root causes of our distraction, we will continue to find ways to distract ourselves.

Scheduling time to 'waste'

Another important idea that Eyal shared with me is that the time you plan to waste is not wasted time. Let me say that again: time you plan to waste is not wasted time. It's perfectly okay to spend time watching TV in the evenings, but it all comes down to doing it with intention. If you put time aside in your calendar to watch TV, then suddenly you'll be doing exactly what you planned and not simply mindlessly scrolling.

I used to feel that the weekend wasn't a 'success' unless I could rattle off a list of things I'd done. Only once I realised that (a) no-one cared, (b) I was trying to meet an arbitrary measure of success and (c) I was exhausted, did I finally allow myself to do things that weren't necessarily 'productive'. It turns out that walking and talking with a friend for hours with no plan or agenda fills my cup the most – so that's what I prioritise now. It comes down to figuring out how you actually want to spend your time, not how you think you should.

Improving your digital life

Cal Newport writes in *Digital Minimalism* that 'the key to thriving in our high-tech world is to spend much less time using technology', but that's much easier said than done. We spend a huge amount of our lives online these days, including an average of at least two hours on social media every single day. It's no wonder that the content we see online shapes our thoughts, feelings and opinions. Suddenly, we're comparing ourselves to the digital presence of people from across the globe we've never met and shaping our views of issues according to our feeds.

Social media can be a great tool for connection, self-expression and learning, but it has its downsides, including being linked to lower quality of sleep, greater comparison and increased mental health issues. So, here's an idea. Whether it's by eliminating ads, focusing on content from friends or family or just increasing the number of cute bunny videos on your Instagram feed, use your time to curate a better digital experience for yourself. Here are some ideas to kickstart your improved digital life:

- Install an ad-blocker on your web browser.
- Use a program to set time limits on or block certain apps and websites.

- Unfollow or mute social media accounts from brands and people you don't know. You can also mute accounts that you find yourself in a constant comparison trap with – they won't even know!
- Actively follow accounts with content that makes you happy or engages your interests. (For example, I love to see content about books.)
- Unsubscribe from marketing emails.
- Declutter your inbox by moving emails into folders, using auto-responses when necessary, and adding auto-forward rules and filters to your inbox.
- Follow accounts that will challenge and expand your views. It's important (especially as an investor) not to end up in an echo chamber.

✎ Identify one change you can make today to improve your online experience and reduce distractions. Now make that change and reflect on whether any of the other strategies could make a difference to your digital experience.

Remember, technology is just a tool. You get to decide how to use it. Don't let all your time get sucked up by distractions. Find ways to manage the noise and spend your time intentionally.

TL;DR

- Your time matters and it shouldn't be discounted as a resource for buying happiness in your life. If you prioritise having more time over more money, you might just end up happier. Remember, time is a finite resource; once you spend it, you can't get it back.
- Your time is an asset that can be converted into money, achievements, better relationships and more choices, depending on how you spend it.

- Consider how you're allocating your time right now and whether it aligns with your values. By conducting a life audit, you can assess the difference between how you're currently spending your time and how you'd like to be spending it – and then start working towards that ideal.
- Research shows that you might be happier if you prioritise time over money, and one way to do this is by outsourcing tasks you dislike.
- Regret doesn't have to be a negative feeling. Rather, you could consider it proof that you've grown as a person and want to spend your time differently today.
- Use technology intentionally and as a tool to improve your life. Don't let it take time away from you.

7

Buying happiness

Maximise your enjoyment of life

In life we must choose our regrets. Rather than working out which decision you want to live with, imagine which decision you couldn't bear living without. Which regrets could you put up with having chosen, and which could you never forgive yourself for?
Morgan Housel

Time stopped when Ed Sheeran came on stage at the Melbourne Cricket Ground, and for two hours the 108,000 of us in that stadium forgot about our day-to-day worries and just sang our hearts out. For the price of admission, I'd argue that every one of us had successfully bought an evening of pure unbridled happiness – and it was worth every cent.

In 2022 I read Elizabeth Dunn, Daniel Gilbert and Timothy Wilson's paper 'If money doesn't make you happy then you probably aren't spending it right' after Ali Abdaal, one of my favourite YouTubers, discussed it on his channel. Something clicked for me when I read that research. I'd known there was something to the idea of buying happiness because I'd seen it in action in the lives of friends, family and my podcast community. I'd experienced it myself at that

Ed Sheeran concert. However, this paper drew together a huge list of studies and gave me proof of what I'd long suspected: money can make you happy if you learn to spend it right.

Let's face it. There's no point paying off debt, saving and building wealth, and then getting to the end of your life without ever really living on your own terms or figuring out what makes you happy. That's what we're aiming for when getting our finances in order: not financial independence for the sake of it, but to create a life in which we get to choose how we spend our time and money, or at least spend it a little better.

In this chapter I'm going to take a look at the relationship between money and happiness, explore ways that money can be used to buy happiness, and point out some important things to keep an eye on as you progress on your wealth-building journey. While I can't promise you that if you increase your personal wealth you'll never be unhappy again, I can show you some research-backed methods to increase your overall happiness levels using money.

Money and happiness

You wouldn't be surprised by the statement 'Higher levels of income lead to lower stress levels', would you? Having studied this in detail, Harvard Business School professor Jon Jachimowicz explains, 'it's not that rich people don't have problems, but having money allows you to fix problems and resolve them more quickly'. In his study, he got participants with incomes ranging from US$10,000 to $150,000+ to keep a diary for 30 days and record their emotional responses to events. Based on the data he gathered, Jachimowicz drew the following conclusions:

1. Money reduces intense stress, especially around negative events.
2. Having more money brings us greater control over our daily lives.
3. People with higher incomes are generally more satisfied with their lives.

Money doesn't stop bad things from happening, but it definitely makes them a little easier to deal with. You can make sure that when you're dealing with the worst day of your life, you don't have to worry about money as well – and that matters. This elimination (or at least reduction) of immediate financial stress is one of the most valuable things that can be achieved with money.

Remember our discussion about emergency funds in chapter 1? That's a key piece of the happiness puzzle. Having an emergency fund that can be used when the unexpected happens or being able to take a day off work to support a friend when they really need us are both examples of how money can make challenging experiences in life more manageable. Having additional money also makes the little things easier, like being able to pay for a ride home when the train is cancelled or being able to pay for groceries to be delivered.

To help you make life's challenges more manageable, in coming chapters I'm going to show you ways to invest and start building wealth. My ambition is that the money you'll make as a result will help you to reduce your stress, gain greater control in your life and increase your overall life satisfaction.

First, however, I want to explore what I have learned about the ways money can be used to buy happiness. Of course, the more money you have, the more easily you'll be able to use these strategies, but you might be surprised by the differences that some small intentional changes to how you spend your money can make to your happiness. Let's explore some practical ways you can start using the money you have right now to add value to your life.

Smoothing the road ahead

As I mentioned in the previous chapter, it's possible to buy back your time by outsourcing tasks you don't enjoy (or that just drain your time), but what I want to focus on here is the resulting emotional – read: happiness – benefits that you can achieve by smoothing the road ahead with money. In contrast to setting up your emergency fund for dealing with unexpected challenges, this is about using your money to make your daily life easier, which can reduce the stress and add happiness to your day. For example, I took my work shirts to the dry cleaner this week, which saved me having to hand wash and risk burning them with my ironing skills.

Here's my challenge to you. Think about how you can spend your money to smooth your road ahead. If you have money to spare in your budget, pick one thing to experiment with this week – whether it's getting a jacket dry cleaned or paying an accountant to do your taxes. This is also a good opportunity to let yourself think bigger and add some goals to your vision board (see chapter 3). For example, though you might not be able to afford it right now, you might like to pay for a cleaner each fortnight in a few years' time.

As I mentioned in chapter 6, it's worth keeping in mind that you don't need to aim to smooth out every bump from your life. Depending on your values and what you enjoy, that could even detract from your happiness! Besides, some of the best stories come from mishaps and misadventures, and there's value in asking for help, connecting with your local community and facing consequences head on.

Experiences > things

One sentence in particular stood out to me in that paper on happiness: 'Money is an opportunity for happiness, but it is an opportunity that people routinely squander because the things they think will make them happy often don't.' Society has trained us well to reach for material items, promising they'll make us happier, but that feeling of excitement when you first buy an item can quickly fizzle out – especially if there wasn't much intention behind the purchase. In contrast, research shows that it's the experiences we purchase that tend to bring us more immediate and longer-lasting happiness.

In *Die With Zero*, Bill Perkins describes the way we relive our memories and the happiness we get from that as 'memory dividends'. Put simply, memory dividends are the ongoing doses of happiness we experience every time we think back on an experience, such as a special vacation. Not only do you get the benefit of the experience the first time around; it also lives on for years in your memories. I know I've felt the effects of this, because when the magic of seeing Ed Sheeran on stage eventually ended – and everyone went home, the happiness I experienced during that event wasn't over. In fact, it still brings me happiness reflecting back on this memory today.

The ability to adapt quickly is typically considered to be one of humanity's greatest skills; however, in contributing to the phenomenon of hedonic adaptation, it can have a huge negative impact on our finances. *Psychology Today* defines 'hedonic adaptation' as the 'process by which positive or negative effects on happiness fade over time'. Essentially, we might think a pay rise will make us happier, and it probably will the first time, but if we're not careful, we'll quickly adapt our spending to our new salary level and face similar struggles to those we did before. One way to combat hedonic adaptation is to focus less on buying material items and more on purchasing experiences, because we don't adapt as quickly to new experiences.

Something we don't pay as much attention to is the role that experiences play in connecting us with others and developing our relationships. Often experiences are shared with friends or family (for example, going to a concert or having Christmas lunch) or allow us to meet new people (such as joining a local netball team or taking evening classes). Research also shows that this social element increases how much happiness we get out of experiences, so bear this in mind as you plan your next adventure or activity.

Sometimes material items can also be experiences, and there's what researchers call a 'fuzzy boundary between these two types of purchases'. However, most consumers were able to categorise their past purchase into one of the categories. Take the books written by my favourite author, Sarah J. Maas, for example. Over the years I have anticipated her book releases, devoured them within days, talked about them with other fans and experienced it all over again by rereading the series years later. These one-off purchases have resulted in significant memory dividends over the years. This shows that money spent on some material items can also be considered investments in happiness, particularly if those purchases will pay ongoing memory dividends.

Although there's a lot of research telling us to pursue memories over attic fillers, we often struggle to put this into practice because we don't really stop to think about what purchases – be that of experiences or material items – actually make us happy. So, let's work on that now.

✎ Make a list of your five biggest material item purchases over the past year (excluding things like rent and utilities) and a second list of your five biggest experiential purchases over the past year. Then reflect on these questions:

- How do you feel looking at and thinking about each list?
- What brings back more memories and feelings of happiness?
- What are some ways you could start using your money to add more experiences into your life? (Think about small things, such as taking a friend out to do an activity, as well as bigger vision-board ideas, such going on an overseas family holiday.

Anticipation is half the fun

Think about the times in life when you've anticipated an event or getting something you really want for hours, days or even weeks in advance. In the lead-up, you're visualising your summer holiday, imagining your lifestyle in a new house or dreaming about finally getting to visit the restaurant you've heard such good things about. Despite the possibility of feeling nervous, impatient or annoyed while you wait, research shows that the more you anticipate an experience, the more enjoyment and satisfaction you get from it.

This effect is much more evident in anticipating experiences than anticipating acquiring material items. Plus, anticipating positive events in your future is great for your mental health. One study showed that 'anticipating a positive event is sufficient to induce a positive emotional state' and allows us to deal with stresses in our life more easily.

✎ Have a look at your calendar. Are there any events coming up over the next six months that you're looking forward to? This could be a lunch with a friend, a work conference or a concert you've booked tickets to. If there's not, can you book something that you're going to look forward to?

On top of the happiness-boosting benefits of anticipating future experiences, delaying purchases is typically much better for your finances than purchasing impulsively, on credit or using BNPL services. The message we get from retailers, banks and BNPL companies is that you deserve it, so don't worry about saving up! Buy it right now. However, that message only serves them at the end of the day.

Let's reverse BNPL by saving up now and buying later if we still feel like it; save now buy later, if you will. The next time you've got your eye on something specific, try this: instead of buying on credit or dipping into your savings: create a goal, open a designated account, work out how much you can reasonably put aside each month and then automate this plan so it happens in the background. Give yourself time to really think about it, visualise and enjoy the build-up of anticipation before you even purchase the experience or item.

Spending on others

How much money do you invest in your relationships with friends and family? Research suggests that we're a lot happier when we spend money on others than we are when we spend that same amount on ourselves. Unfortunately, research also shows that we often get this wrong, believing that we'd be happier spending that money on ourselves.

One of the reasons why spending money on friends and family makes us happier is that it can help with building social ties. Just think about how you feel when you alternate paying for coffee or lunch with a friend. It's an implicit arrangement, in a way, that you'll catch up again soon. It demonstrates that you trust they will continue the pattern. Think about how you feel when buying gifts for loved ones (especially surprise ones) or donating money to organisations that matter to you. These actions can create stronger ties to your community and bring you much more happiness than spending the same amount of money on yourself.

It's definitely easier to be generous with money when you aren't on a tight budget. Spontaneous dinners out, big gifts and giving money to family, friends and charity are all a lot easier when you have more money. If your budget is tight right now, consider ways to express generosity and strengthen connections that won't negatively affect your path to getting out of debt or building your emergency fund. For example, this might be having friends over for coffee instead of going out, or perhaps using your time to help a family member set up furniture.

Does all this generosity have a downside? Think about your generosity like a water tank. If you just leave the tap running all the time, chances are it'll run out before the rain comes to fill it up again. You need to look after yourself as well. Plus, if your tank runs out, you can't help anyone.

How can you use your money (or time) to connect with or support your friends and family this week? Can you surprise your mum with flowers, buy your friend a coffee or take their dog for a walk? Pick one thing and give it a go, then reflect on how that made you feel.

Giving money away

Consider how you can share the resources you have with others, because this has a big impact on happiness. In his popular TEDx Talk, Michael Norton from Harvard Business School shares that spending money on other people makes us happy. He goes on to say that the benefits don't come just on grand acts of generosity, such as donating $10,000 to a local school. The small acts have just as much of an impact on your happiness: for example, spending money at the school fair, buying someone a coffee or donating $50 to a fundraiser online.

Norton also highlighted a 2008–09 survey conducted by the Gallup World Poll that found in 120 of 136 countries, individuals who donated to charity in the previous month reported higher levels of life satisfaction. One point to note with this research, says the University of Oxford's Andreas Mogensen, is the importance of knowing how an organisation is going to use your money. According to the research, the happiness boost is greater when it's clear exactly how the money helps others.

Many of us want to give more to others but don't feel we have the time to do so. One way to change this is by prioritising it in your budget through a regular direct debit arrangement with a charitable organisation or allocating $100 a month in your budget for giving to others. You could also consider using organisations like The Life You Can Save, founded by moral philosopher Peter Singer, who do the research for you in finding the most effective places for you to donate your money.

✎ Challenge yourself to give away $10 in the next 24 hours, perhaps by paying it forward, putting some coins in the tip jar or donating to charity, and reflect on how it makes you feel.

The effects of quantity and novelty

Sometimes lots of low-cost experiences and purchases can be better than one more expensive one. Although those big experiences such as overseas holidays are fantastic, they might mean less money for happiness-boosting purchases throughout the year. This comes back to the idea of hedonic adaptation, whereby the brain adapts quickly to one big experience or purchase, but is slower to adapt to more regular ones. After we sleep off the jet lag from our big trip, we're quickly looking for the next boost of happiness.

I make the choice to buy coffee with friends on the weekends because I find that act brings me more happiness and contentedness – not just in the moment, but also throughout the week – than I feel I would get if I spent that money on a weekend away once a year. It comes back to your values, goals and preferences, though, so it's worth experimenting with this idea. Think about low-cost ways of providing yourself with regular happiness boosts. This might look like a weekly exercise class with friends, purchasing a new book once a month or trying a new cafe each weekend.

Another way you may be able to elevate the happiness that money can buy is by mixing up how and what you spend your money on. According to the experts, you can use the following variables to improve your brain's perception of an experience:

- novelty (you haven't experienced it before)
- surprise (you didn't expect it to happen)
- uncertainty (you're not entirely sure what it is)
- variability (it keeps changing).

One obvious way to apply the theory of novelty to buying happiness is to do new and interesting things with your money – visiting a country you haven't been to before, for example, or skydiving if you've never done it – but don't forget our discussion about quantity. Even if you're doing something small, such as going out for coffee on the weekend, you can still introduce an element of novelty to improve your experience. For example, you could go to a new coffee shop, shout your friend a coffee or change up the time of day. You'd still be spending a similar amount of money, but you'd get a different experience – and you might just enjoy it more.

You can take this a step further by pairing up with a friend. Alternating each month, one of you could book a surprise activity, giving the other just the time, location and dress code. This a great way to mix things up and have experiences you might not have chosen on your own.

✎ Think about some ways you can spend your money differently to add more novelty to and increase the quantity of your purchases.

This is one way to take the money you're already spending on your wants each month, making some small tweaks and getting an extra happiness boost from it.

What money *doesn't* buy

After reading some of the research-backed strategies in this chapter, you might be thinking, 'That's all well and good Kate, but money can't buy everything; it doesn't buy me a good relationship with my sister, the years I lost to health issues or a feeling of satisfaction with my life.' And I would agree with you. There's a lot that money can't buy, and these things are important to focus on as well.

Having spoken to friends and family of all ages, I've compiled a selection of things that money can't buy here. Take some time to reflect on how these, and any other similarly invaluable things, play out in your own life, and consider how you might be able to address each one.

Health

Ill-health can be caused by a huge range of factors and, although money may allow you to access the level of care required to treat or manage some medical conditions, a lot of issues can't be simply paid off. What you can do with money, however, is use it to look after the body you have right now, in the best way you can; after all, it's the only one you get. If you have the financial resources, consider how you might be able to use them to care proactively for your health, whether that's by engaging in preventative healthcare, not putting off expensive appointments, engaging in fitness activities you enjoy or buying higher quality foods.

Lost time

You can't buy back lost time. Even if you'd change it all, money couldn't buy you a time machine. The way to manage this is to focus on the choices you make going forwards, claiming the moments as they come and using your money to increase the time you have to do things you love – with the people who mean the most to you. Reflect on some of the ideas covered in chapter 6 to consider how you might be able to manage feelings of regret and spend your time more intentionally from this point onwards.

Quality relationships

A study of undergraduate students in the USA found that the happiest students were very social and had stronger relationships than the less happy students. The researchers pointed out that the happy students didn't 'experience more objectively defined good events' or have any significant commonalities aside from their strong social relationships. You might be able to buy friendship for a short period of time, if you're shouting all the rounds and buying lavish gifts, but they aren't the kind of friendships that'll stand the test of time. It takes time, effort and showing up on a regular basis to build quality relationships. The kind of connections that mean the people you care about will show up for your best and worst moments take time to develop, and they can't be bought. As the classic saying goes, people remember how you made them feel, so don't neglect building quality relationships on your quest to reaching other financial goals.

Purpose

We're commonly told that if we find and follow our purpose, we'll never work a day in our lives. I have a lot of issues with that advice, but I'd argue that living your days with purpose and intention isn't something you can write a cheque for. You have to figure out for yourself what your priorities are in life and how you want to spend your time. It's not something that anyone else can solve for you. It's another aspect of your life that you figure out with time, experience and experimentation.

Feeling content

The feeling of having – and being – enough and being satisfied with your life and what you have is one of the most important things that money can't buy. There are enough examples of unhappy celebrities and billionaire entrepreneurs alone to show that. If you can't find satisfaction with what you have now, it's still going to be hard to find it if you have more money, things and time. Remember, it's likely that you once wanted what you have now. Finding a way to be grateful at each point along your journey is critical to your overall happiness.

✎ Ask yourself what you can do right now that will move you one step closer to the person you want to be and the life you want to live. You don't need to put this off to a later date. Start now.

How I buy happiness

Someone once told me if you're asking yourself whether you're happy, there's a good chance you're not completely happy. Still, I think a little self-reflection and proactiveness in this area of life can be a very good thing. Writing this book has pushed me to slow down and think about all the ways I've bought happiness in my life: through experiences, material items and just the time to slow down with loved ones.

Reflecting on how I've bought happiness recently, I can see that I've made a few big purchases that have been worth every cent for the happiness they brought, including a month-long solo travel experience through Europe, tickets to live performances, gifts for friends and family, and two new bookshelves. Some of these bigger items, such as going overseas, required setting goals and saving up for months or years in advance. I needed to get a handle on my spending, manage my budget, increase my income and get comfortable with delayed gratification. Having spent the time working out my values and priorities, when I made those purchases, I was confident they would make me happy – and they did. However, it's worth remembering that bigger and more expensive doesn't necessarily mean better. There are lots of smaller things I've also enjoyed in that time for little or even no cost, such as reading a good book, walking in nature, sharing a freshly brewed pot of tea with a friend and chatting on the phone with my parents.

✎ My challenge to you now is to write a list on your phone of small, inexpensive things that make you happy. Then, when you're having a tough day or you just need a pick-me-up, pull out your list and tick off one of those activities.

It's fascinating to hear about how other people have bought happiness in their own lives, and if the idea is completely new to you, it can also be really helpful to hear other perspectives. So, I put the call out to my community for ways they've bought happiness recently. I've included a sample of their responses at the back of this book in case you're in need of a little inspiration, and you can find even more ideas online at buyinghappiness.com.au.

TL;DR

This chapter started out with the proposition that if money doesn't make you happy then you're probably not spending it right. If you combine using your time with intention (as discussed in chapter 6) with some of the strategies I set out in this chapter, it's likely that you'll be able to boost your happiness. Wanting to be able to buy happiness is a great reason for getting your finances in order. We've set some strong foundations, and now we're going to explore how to get your money working harder so you can reach bigger financial goals – such as becoming financially independent – by adding in investing to your plan.

- Money can make us feel more in control, reduce feelings of intense stress and help us feel more satisfied with our lives.
- We tend to get a bigger happiness boost from using money to purchase experiences than we do material items.

- By sharing our resources and spending our money on others, including friends, family and charitable organisations, we feel happier than if we spend the money on ourselves.
- Though it can help, money can't buy happiness in some areas of life, such as health, relationships and purpose. Pursuing wealth at the expense of these can make us feel less happy, so be careful not to lose sight of what's important.

8

From little things big things grow

Understand compound interest, start investing and automate your financial future

... the average person needs only two things to become wealthy: the knowledge of what to do, and the discipline to do those things.
Noel Whittaker

As we discussed in the last chapter, money can buy happiness if we spend it well. Although it's not a magic cure for life's challenges, having it can make things that little bit easier. It stands to reason that we'd want to make more of it, right? So, how do we turn what we've got right now into a pot of gold – without turning into a goblin along the way? I want to introduce you to the idea of investing: why it's a lot easier than it looks, how you can use it to build wealth in a sustainable way and then, most importantly, get on with your life.

This chapter is all about building wealth through investing so you can buy happiness now and in the future. As you'll see, the small steps you take with your money compound over time. By the end of this chapter you'll have opened a brokerage account, invested your first

$5 and begun to automate your financial future – it doesn't have to be hard!

The basics of investing

What comes to mind when you think about the word 'investing'? It feels out of reach for many, like something that only certain people get to do. I want to debunk this idea, because investing isn't about men in suits shouting at each other on the trading floor anymore. Investing is accessible to anyone, and it can play a big role in helping you achieve your financial goals – be that spending more time with family, taking time away from work to travel, paying off a mortgage or having more security in retirement. It's all about planting trees today that will provide you with shade in decades to come.

So, what does investing actually mean? Let's keep things as simple as possible. When you invest, you're buying something that other people value with the expectation that you'll be able to sell it for a higher price in the future. It's common for new investors to start by researching and purchasing shares in a company or units in an exchange traded fund (ETF), so I'm going to give you some information about both in this chapter that you can use as a starting point. Although I won't be focusing on them in this book, there are plenty of other investment options available to you, too, including property and bonds. These can all form part of your portfolio, so make sure to look into them as well using the resources I've included at the end of this book.

✎ There are many different things you can invest in, but let's stick with a company to start with. Think about a company that you love to use the products and services of on a regular basis. Write it down. Now I want you to put your research skills to the test. What kind of details can you find out about the company? Think about the following:

- where their headquarters are
- who the CEO is

- how many employees they have
- recent media articles they've been featured in
- the different products and services they sell
- what countries they operate in
- any financial data they've released.

If you were able to answer some of these questions, well done! These are some of the very high-level details that professional investment analysts would include in their research process. When you invest in shares, you're simply buying a slice of a company. In one single transaction, you can become the owner of a tiny slice of a business. How cool is that?! (Heads up: when you're researching, you might see the word 'stock' used instead of 'share', but don't worry – for our purposes they mean the same thing.)

Not all companies are publicly traded and may instead be held by just a few investors. The company you researched, for example, might've been your local cafe, which probably just has a handful of owners and would be more challenging to buy (unless you feel like running a café, that is). However, you might've been researching a company like Disney, which is publicly traded on the New York Stock Exchange (NYSE). More on that in a moment.

What I hope you gathered from this process is that, in most cases, a company does something. They create and sell products or services, employ staff, pay taxes, market themselves, and research and develop new ideas. If things go to plan, they will grow; through selling more products and services, hiring more staff, becoming more well-known and raising prices. By investing in a growing company, you generally benefit as a shareholder over time as the company's share price increases. For example, you might buy 100 shares of a company at $10 each, valuing your total investment at $1000. If the share price of the company increases to $12, the total value of your investment would be worth $1200. Of course, the opposite can happen, too. Using the same example, if the share price falls to $8, the value of your investment would fall to $800.

Although the share market goes up and down every day (remember those finance news updates on the TV), the outcomes are significantly less random over time, and education and research play a major role in your results. Plus, smart investors (like you and I) never put all their money into a single investment, because diversification is an effective strategy for reducing your risks. Just think, if you put 100 per cent of your money in one company that went bankrupt, you might end up with $0; however, if you own 20 different companies, one company failing won't have a huge effect on your portfolio overall. If this all sounds a little complicated, don't worry; I'm going to explore another tool to help with this, the ETF, later in this chapter.

Investing isn't gambling

Before we go any further, I need to clarify that investing, particularly in the way I'm going to explain shortly, isn't gambling. The Australian Institute of Family Studies estimates that Australians lose about $25 billion on legal gambling every year, which is an absolutely shocking amount. If you or a loved one is impacted by gambling, there are specialist support services available, including the Gambling Help Online website in Australia, which provides free and confidential support.

When you gamble, you're playing a random game of chance in which the system is set up for you to lose. Consider this, when you gamble and lose money, the casino makes money, so it's in their interests to manipulate the odds against you. In contrast, when you buy shares in a company, both parties want the same thing: for the company to grow, which drives the share price up over time. This means your incentives are aligned.

All that said, you can invest with a gambling mentality, which is where things get dicey. We call this 'speculating'. You've probably heard of a friend sinking a huge portion of their savings into an investment they heard about at a party or on Reddit without doing any research (think about the crypto craze that swept the internet). They might have struck gold and made a small fortune, but it's much more likely that they lost a significant amount of money. Engaging in speculation is a reliable way to lose sleep and part with some of your money – hardly the best way to buy happiness! But that's not going to be your story. You're going to take a slow and steady approach to investing and focus on diversifying your portfolio, investing on a regular basis and making sure you understand where you're putting your money.

The magic snowball: Compound interest

I'm sure you've seen something before that made you think, 'That's impossible!' Perhaps it was a 500-year-old tree, a rainbow stretching across a valley or one of the incredible illusions on Netflix's *Magic for Humans*. Even when you understand the science or the mechanism, the magic remains. That's how I still sometimes feel about compound interest, which is the mechanism by which the money I invest grows over time.

Think of a savings account, for example. You might have $1000 in that account earning an interest rate of 3 per cent. At the end of the year, you'll have around $1030 in your account. Then in the second year you'll be earning 3 per cent on your increased balance of $1030. Basically, you're earning interest on your interest, which continues to grow – to compound – over time.

At its core, compound interest is a way to describe how money makes more money over time, but it's best illustrated through an example. (We'll leave out fees and taxes to keep things simple.) Let's say you invest $1000 a month for 30 years. If you invest your money in a diversified portfolio with an average annual return of 7 per cent, the expected value of the investments in your portfolio would be over $1,000,000 after 30 years. Your contribution to this sum over the 30 years is $360,000, but the rest is made up of capital growth and any income you receive from your investments.

Let's break it down. Capital growth occurs when the value of your investment goes up, and is now worth more than you initially paid for it. So, if I purchased a share for $5 and it's now $10, that's $5 of capital growth. Investment income is paid when the company pays out some of the profits to you as an investor. This payment is called a dividend and forms part of your overall return on the investment, though not every company pays income to investors.

Compare the results of investing to what would happen if you put your $1000 each month into a savings account instead of investing it. Your contribution over the 30 years would still be $360,000, but with an average interest rate of 3 per cent, you would only have about $580,000 after all that time. Still a lot of money, but you don't get to benefit from capital growth when your money is in a savings account, and it will take you much longer to build wealth.

Table 2 breaks this calculation down to show what different monthly investments can turn into over different timeframes with the help of compound interest. Two things stand out in this table. First, the longer you're able to invest for, the better your results will be. Second, the more you're able to invest, the faster you're able to build wealth. Remember, you might start with investing $100 a month, but over time as you increase your income, you can increase this amount. The more fuel you can add to the engine of compound interest, the larger your investment portfolio will grow over time, ultimately giving you more choice about what you do with your time. Don't let these big numbers put you off, though; the most important thing is to get started. I'd really encourage you to look at a compound interest calculator (you can find a simple one at moneysmart.gov.au) to get a better feel for how compound interest works – and particularly how just a little bit can end up making a big difference.

You might be wondering how an investment portfolio worth $1,000,000 will help you buy happiness in the future, and it's a great question. Not only does this investment portfolio provide you with financial security; you can actually turn it into money in the bank

Table 2: Compound interest and monthly investments

	5 years	10 years	15 years	20 years	25 years	30 years
$100/month	$6900	$16,600	$30,200	$49,200	$75,900	$113,400
$250/month	$17,300	$41,400	$75,400	$123,000	$189,700	$283,400
$500/month	$34,500	$82,900	$150,800	$246,000	$379,500	$566,800
$1000/month	$69,000	$165,800	$301,500	$491,900	$759,000	$1,133,500
$2000/month	$138,000	$331,600	$603,100	$983,900	$1,518,000	$2,267,100
$3000/month	$207,000	$497,400	$904,600	$1,475,800	$2,277,000	$3,400,600

Note: These numbers have been rounded to the nearest $100 and assume an average annual return of 7 per cent, disregarding fees and taxes.

account to pay for bills, overseas holidays and so on. While the best way to do this is something you should chat to an accountant about (there's always tax to be mindful of), you've got two main options. You can sell some of your investments (capital growth) or you can spend the income you receive from your investments. We'll discuss this more in chapter 10, but building wealth means you have choices, now and in 30 years' time.

The idea of compounding growth isn't just about money: small actions in every area of your life compound over time. Think of your relationships, fitness, education, mental health and career. Getting used to the idea that the choices you consistently make today have a massive impact ten, 20 and 30 years down the road is important. Sometimes it's hard to prioritise your future self because things feel uncertain and far away. So, I want you to try visualising yourself in 30 years' time. What are you doing? Where are you living? What relationships are important to you? What makes you happy? If you want future-you to have all that, what actions can you start taking today to get there?

Investing isn't as hard as you think

If this is all feeling like a lot right now, you're not alone. Many people stop at this point, just before they get to the life-changing stuff. That's not an overstatement; investing and building wealth does change lives – for generations to come. It's worth persevering with, and I promise you, once you know the basics, you're sorted!

The principles of investing haven't changed for hundreds of years. Companies come and go, and so does the technology that allows you to invest in them, but the mindset of investing to build wealth will stay with you for a lifetime. Investing doesn't need to become your life – or even your hobby. You'll never have to sit at home in front of five computer screens looking at share price charts. In fact, very few people invest that way. As you're probably aware, humans love to overcomplicate even the simplest of things, and the finance industry is no exception.

Before we go any further, make sure you've worked through the foundations set out in chapters 1 and 2. If you're not sure or you've skipped ahead, go back now and complete those essential first steps. It's important to sort out expensive debts and make sure you've got your emergency fund organised first. If you've covered all that, congratulations – you're ready to invest! To empower you to get started, I've distilled everything I've learnt from experts and everyday people who have used the principles of investing to build a nest egg for their family into five simple steps. Together we'll make your very first investment – even if it's just $5 – and then you'll be on your way!

Step 1: Find a brokerage account

Before we jump into the exciting stuff, you'll need to open a brokerage account. A brokerage account connects you with buyers and sellers of investments. The broker is basically the go-between; you tell them what you want and how much you want to pay, and they go and collect all the goods for you, process the payment and hold your things until you want to sell them or transfer them somewhere else. This all happens in seconds and generally doesn't cost very much.

Start your search for a brokerage account by googling 'Top brokerage accounts Australia' and then use the results as a springboard to research your options. Be aware that some comparison sites don't include every option, and that they may receive incentives for listing some brokerage accounts higher than others, so make sure to look at multiple sources and consider your unique needs.

Some of the features to compare when choosing a brokerage account include the following:

- **Fees:** These could range from $3 to $20 each time you buy or sell an investment, depending on the broker. I'll discuss brokerage fees a little later.

- **Minimum investment:** Can you invest with $5, or is the minimum $500? If you want to start investing with smaller amounts of money, you'll need to check the platform's minimum investment.
- **User experience:** Is the platform easy for you to use and understand? You need to feel comfortable making investments on the platform. If having a good phone app is important to you, make sure to test it out.
- **Reporting:** Does the platform generate helpful reports for you at tax time and provide data on your performance? Anything that helps make your life easier as an investor is a great feature, especially as you get further into your investing journey.
- **Security:** Is your account protected by at least two layers of security? Given the rise in hacking and scams, you'll want to make sure your investments are safe. Find out what security features you can enable on your account. Make sure you choose a broker that is regulated and authorised.
- **Markets:** What investments does the platform allow you to buy? The most common exchanges investors want to access are the NASDAQ and NYSE for buying shares in US-listed companies and of course the ASX for buying shares in Australian-listed companies.

Try out a few different brokerage platforms and see what you feel comfortable using. I suggest jumping back to the analysis paralysis section in chapter 4, which walks you through the process of deciding which brokerage account to use if you're getting stuck. Before you fully commit, my number one tip is to test drive the brokerage account you're considering to make sure it's straightforward to use before you make your first investment. It's a very individual decision, so give it a go! You can then close down any accounts you decide not to use. It's that easy.

A note on fees

Brokerage fees can be charged as a flat fee (for example, $9.50) or a percentage of the investment value (for example, 0.12 per cent). While it's important to keep fees low an investor, so that more of your money goes to building wealth, don't choose your brokerage account based on fees alone. Make sure to consider all the factors I listed when selecting the right platform for you. In addition to brokerage, which is a normal fee charged by all brokers, you could be paying account keeping fees or fees for extra services that you don't use. Don't be afraid to shop around. Many brokerage accounts don't charge ongoing account fees, while for others, fees are optional for extra features.

Step 2: Research different investments

The next challenge after opening a brokerage account is deciding what to invest in. This is a tough step because it's so personal! Everyone who reads this book has different values, goals and priorities, and as a result will choose to invest in different things. That's part of what makes investing so interesting, but it can also be something that stops us from getting started.

It's tempting to hold out for something that's exactly right, but I want you to remember as you work through this section that there just isn't a perfect portfolio that will suit everyone. The way I invest will look different to the way you choose to invest, but there are similar steps we can both take to research potential investments. To make things as straightforward as possible, I'm going to focus on explaining shares and ETFs, and give you some practical tips you can use to make your own investment decisions. If you want to dive in deeper, head to the resources section at the end of the book, where I've included some free tools to help you learn more.

Shares

As I covered a little earlier in this chapter, shares simply represent ownership of a company. The most important thing to keep in mind is that when you buy a share, you're buying a slice of a business. In Australia, publicly traded companies are listed on the Australian Securities Exchange (ASX). This means that you can buy a slice of large Australian companies like BHP, CBA, CSL, Wesfarmers or Telstra through your brokerage account.

Many investors choose to invest in individual shares as they believe they can outperform. Outperform what? Good question. One reference point an investor might use here is the S&P/ASX 200 index, which tracks the largest 200 Australian companies listed on the ASX. An investor might buy a selection of different top-200 businesses that they think will perform well instead of simply investing in all the top-200 companies through an ETF (more on that shortly). Selecting the companies today that will be the winners tomorrow, when there are over 2000 to choose from on the ASX alone, is quite the challenge – even the experts struggle with it.

Another reason for investing in shares is the ability to be very selective about where your money is invested. You can research and learn about what a company does before you invest your money in it. Some of the things that investors look at before choosing a company include the annual report, background and experience of the board, CEO and management team, financial statements, customer and employee feedback, and who the main competitors are. Basically, what makes this company better than the others someone could invest in, and why they think it will grow in value over time.

Share investing can be a good option, but it does take a lot of time to do well. This stops many investors from getting started, as they don't have the time, knowledge or desire to properly research a company. But that doesn't mean you can't be a great investor. If you're looking for something less time intensive and easier to start with, let me tell you about ETFs.

Exchange traded funds

One of the best inventions in the world of money is the exchange traded fund (ETF). An ETF is basically a bunch of investments (for example, shares) thrown into a basket based on a set of rules or similar characteristics. For example, the largest 200 companies on the ASX, or a group of technology companies. The set of rules are normally based on tracking an index, which shows the performance of a group of shares. I like to explain it as being similar to a box of Cadbury Favourites. In one single purchase I get a bit of all the chocolates in the box, without having to decide if I want a Crunchie or a Cherry Ripe or something else to the exclusion of other chocolates. When you purchase an ETF, you buy units in a fund, and the ETF provider purchases and manages the underlying investments on your behalf.

To give you a practical example, the S&P 500 index tracks the share performance (price) of the 500 largest US-listed companies, such as Apple, Google and Mastercard. Instead of having to manually purchase shares in individual companies, using an ETF that tracks the S&P 500 (such as the IVV ETF) allows you to invest in all of those companies. The value of that ETF then goes up or down in line with the index (and underlying basket of companies) it tracks – to clarify, in the case of the IVV ETF, that's the 500 largest US-listed companies.

The modern-day ETF arrived in the 1990s and has been gaining traction with investors globally ever since. In 2022 it was estimated that there were over 8700 ETFs available globally, providing investors with low-cost ways to invest in an array of assets. You can buy an ETF that invests in just about anything these days, including the top Australian companies, emerging economies and bonds. ETFs are created, packaged up and maintained by ETF managers (biggest names include iShares, Vanguard, BetaShares, VanEck and SPDR), and in exchange they take a small management fee.

One of the great things about ETFs is that they provide you with a way to invest in many things through one fund, which helps keep you diversified. Diversification is the idea that you spread your money across multiple investments, which reduces the risk that you'll lose a significant amount of your money if an investment goes wrong. Using ETFs also reduces your costs (because you don't need to make so many individual purchases) and means you can spend more time living your life, as you don't need to stay up to date on what any one company is doing. ETFs are also transparent; when you start researching them, you'll see that they provide you with a list of everything they invest in.

You can think of ETFs as the building blocks of your portfolio, where you can invest in a range of them to build a portfolio that represents your goals, risk profile and timeframe. ETFs can be used to grow a portfolio in combination with other investments (such as individual shares) or in their own right. For example, in my portfolio I combine ETFs with a range of individual Australian and US shares.

Choosing an ETF

With so many ETFs available to invest in, how do you decide what fits your portfolio? I'm going to break down how you might find some potential options, with the reminder that this isn't an investment recommendation; rather, it's a first step on your own research journey.

Let's say I want to invest in Australian businesses. Instead of buying individual shares in companies like BHP, CBA, CSL, Wesfarmers or Telstra, I want to buy an ETF that does it all for me. I'd start by googling 'Australian shares ETFs' or heading to the large Australian ETF manager websites and make a rough list of my options, such as:

- VAS – Vanguard Australian Shares Index ETF
- IOZ – iShares Core S&P/ASX 200 ETF
- A200 – BetaShares Australia 200 ETF
- STW – SPDR S&P/ASX 200 Fund

Then I'd compare some of the key features between the ETFs. You can do this by looking at similar ETFs and making a note on key attributes like performance. As a long-term investor, it's important to look at three or five-year returns at minimum because this gives a better sense of how the ETF has performed over a long time period. You can also compare the management fees, as some ETFs charge a lot more than others for doing the same thing. Then have a look at what the ETF actually invests in. On the ETFs information page, you can look inside the portfolio using the list of holdings, so you understand what the ETF does. The top holdings for all of the ETFs I just listed will look quite similar, for example, but if you start to look at more niche ETFs that might not be the case.

Before investing, I highly recommend reading the ETF fact sheet and product disclosure statement (PDS), which outlines all the key details and the risks involved. If you don't understand something, give the provider a call and ask them. I promise they've heard them all before and they should be prepared to help you fully understand the key facts. You can also talk to a qualified financial adviser, who can look at your finances and help choose the most suitable investment options for you.

A note on ethical investing

These days we expect more from companies than we used to, and many of us don't want to put our money behind companies involved in activities that go against our values and ethics. This looks different to everyone, but to many that means avoiding companies that are involved in controversial industries such as weapons, tobacco or gambling. Traditionally this has been achieved by only purchasing shares in companies that align with your specific values, but it's now also possible to invest in ETFs that follow a set of rules, such as an ESG (environmental, social and governance) focused portfolio, which excludes certain companies from its list of investments.

Still, it's important not to forget that your ethics are your own. While pre-built strategies, screening techniques and processes can come close to resembling your ethics, you might need to compromise. For example, you might be completely against investing in alcohol companies due to your ethical principles, but it might be difficult to find an ETF on offer that excludes all the industries that you want to avoid. Many of the large ETF providers mentioned earlier in this chapter have their own version of ethical ETFs. You can find more details on their websites about what they offer and how they choose which companies to exclude from their ethical investment products.

Step 3: Purchase your first investment

Now you've opened your brokerage account and know what you want to buy, you can place your order. It's all coming together now!

To make an investment, you need to know the code for the share or ETF (for example, Disney is 'NYSE: DIS'), the price you want to pay for each share and the quantity. You can find the code for the company or ETF you're interested in with a quick Google search or on the ETF provider's website. The price you're prepared to pay for a share in a company is a very individual decision that even experts argue over. Logistically, you have a couple of options: you can place a market order and accept the current price someone is selling for, or you can place a limit order, where your order will only be processed if the value of the share falls below your chosen price. The same process applies when you want to buy an ETF; it'll have its own code, just like a share and you can buy it through the same brokerage account.

Your broker then sends that order to the market and, hopefully, it will be matched with a seller. Your broker will then let you know your order has been processed and arrange settlement automatically. Make sure to check the settlement process and timeframe so you don't get charged any extra fees. You will also need to have the money available in your linked bank account to pay for this purchase, because you're basically exchanging your money for shares in a company.

You can start with just $5

We've covered a lot of ground. If you're feeling overwhelmed right now, I want you to take a breath. Many new investors like to start with a micro-investing app, which keeps things simple and means you can start investing with just $5. Just google 'micro-investing apps in Australia' to explore your options. This can help you get started straight away with a small sum of money and allow you to build up your confidence over time. Just keep an eye out for the fees, which can sometimes be quite high for small balances.

Made it through all these steps? You're officially an investor! But before we move on, there are a few important steps we still need to discuss to turn your first investment into an ongoing wealth-building habit.

Step 4: Automate your financial future

My sister told me when we were discussing her first investments that she wanted to be able to automate her future investments just like her Netflix subscription and phone plan. Step 4 is all about doing just that: automating as much as possible, making saving and investing something that happens in the background and works for you, not against you.

By automating what you can, you can free up time for everything else in life. We've discussed automating in other financial contexts before, but here that could look like automatically transferring a certain amount of money, say $500, into a separate bank account every time you get paid, then investing that money each quarter. Some brokers also allow you to automatically invest in shares or ETFs, so keep an eye out for those helpful tools. The idea is to use technology to give you time, then use that time to be fully present in your life.

✎ I challenge you to find one part of your finances to automate this week, whether that's something related to saving, investing or even keeping on top of your paperwork for tax time. Even a small change will compound over time to have big financial impact.

Step 5: Look after your portfolio

Now you're officially investing on a regular basis, it's important to look after your portfolio. This less fun part of investing is something you'll need to return to reasonably regularly, and includes tax, paperwork, and rebalancing and planning as part of your ongoing portfolio management. Here's a quick rundown of some areas you'll need to stay across.

Being across your tax obligations as an investor is important. Each country's systems will have different requirements, so access resources from your tax office or speak to your accountant to ensure you're compliant. Part of this will likely be staying on top of any paperwork and admin – and not just at tax time. It isn't the most exciting part of investing, but keeping track of what you buy, when you buy it and the price you buy it for is a key part of good investing. This will not only help you make more informed investing decisions and track your performance, but it'll also help you provide accurate data to the tax office.

Another aspect of investing to keep in mind is that some companies pay what's known as a dividend (this may also be called a distribution for some investments). Although companies are not required to pay investors a dividend, some choose to distribute a portion of their profits back to shareholders. Keep an eye out for whether the company or ETF you invest in pays investors a dividend to make sure it's paid out to you on the correct date.

As a guide, once you've set up your portfolio, it's a good idea to put aside time annually (at minimum) for ongoing portfolio management. This essentially means reviewing your portfolio, performance and strategy, and making any changes that you think are necessary. Though you can do this yourself, a financial adviser can assist you with the review process if you need support. An adviser can also help you with the big things like choosing your investment strategy and helping you reach long-term goals (for example, becoming financially independent – more on that in chapter 10).

Now get on with your life

So, there you have it. I hope you can see from this that investing isn't as hard as people make it out to be. Plus, once you know how to invest, you've got this knowledge for life. Although the technology and product availability keeps evolving over time, the basic principles of investing have remained the same. Don't over complicate it – and don't let it take up your entire life!

I can think of a million things I'd rather do on the weekend than look at my investment strategy, but I definitely wasn't like this at the start of my journey. During my first few years of investing, I was learning as much as possible, talking about finance at every chance (so much fun at parties) and looking at my accounts *all the time*. I got a little obsessed, but that doesn't need to be you. As you read earlier, being passionate about and obsessed with money is absolutely *not* necessary to set yourself up for success. All you need is a little bit of effort and patience. You've got this!

TL;DR

If you want to build wealth, investing is one of the best tools you have at your disposal – and it's certainly an area in which a little knowledge gives you a massive leg up. The most important thing is to invest regularly, keep your approach simple (you don't need to get caught up in the hype) and get started today. The more time you have on your side, the easier it is to become financially independent (which we'll unpack in chapter 10). By investing today, you'll have more opportunities to buy happiness in the future and be able to make financial decisions from a position of strength.

- Investing isn't gambling when you focus on building a long-term, low-cost and diversified investment portfolio.

- Don't think of shares as numbers on a screen; think of them as slices of real businesses that have products and services, employees and customers.
- ETFs make it easy to get started with investing, as they bundle up a collection of investments (for example, shares) for you to invest in through your brokerage account.
- Before you commit to a broker, open a few accounts and give them a test run to make sure you feel comfortable with using them.
- Don't forget to look after your portfolio long-term and stay on top of tax, rebalancing and admin tasks.

9

Nothing ventured, nothing gained

Taking risks and making mistakes

Do one thing every day that scares you.
Eleanor Roosevelt

My mum told me that this book wouldn't be complete without mention of the word 'risk' – and she's right, as per usual. You mightn't think the words 'risk' and 'happiness' go together, but I'd like to challenge you on that. Risk is basically the possibility of loss, something that we love to avoid at all costs; however, as we'll discuss in this chapter, taking risks is a big part of your journey to buying happiness.

One study of 20,000 people found that there was a 'strong positive association between life satisfaction and willingness to take risks in general'. Think about some of the best experiences and parts of your life to date, and then consider their origin stories. Did you apply for a job that you weren't sure you were qualified for? Did you ask someone on a date without knowing if they'd say 'yes'? Did you speak up on an issue that affected you or someone else? Did you try an activity that you felt a little apprehensive about? Some of the happiest moments of our lives grow from moments of fear, doubt or worry.

Your investing journey involves taking risks, making mistakes and getting back up again, and growth – in your confidence as an investor and hopefully also in your investments. In this chapter you're going to take a deep dive into understanding what risk looks like to you. You can use this knowledge to inform your decisions as an investor, as the better you understand the role risk plays in investing – and what that means to you – the better you'll be able to make long-term investment decisions. We'll also discuss some strategies to avoid common investing mistakes and how to pick yourself up if you do make one.

What does risk mean to you?

Growing up in regional Australia, I was constantly encouraged to take risks, fall over and keep going. When I was ten years old I begged my parents for singing lessons. I was given a challenge: sing something at the talent contest happening at the local fair and I'd get the lessons I was so keen on. If I didn't have the guts to do that, they weren't going to pay. A bit of tough love for a kid, I have to say, but it worked. I sang a slightly off-key a cappella version of 'Wouldn't it be loverly' from *My Fair Lady*, and my parents kept their word.

This turned into a life of pushing myself out of my comfort zone and getting very comfortable with making mistakes, especially in public. All of this paid off when I started investing because, without worrying about everything that could go wrong, I just started – and as I've shared, getting started is often the hardest part. Sure, it would be some time before I actually put a plan in place and started thinking with a long-term mindset, but that first step was what I needed to kickstart my investing journey.

Much like how our childhood influences our attitudes to money (as discussed in chapter 3), healthy experiences of risk and risk-taking early in life is shown to build resilience and self-esteem that last well into adulthood. Additionally, experiencing loss can help us to understand that actions can have positive and negative consequences.

Some studies have also found that if parents are less willing to take risks, it's likely that's the case for their children as well. So, let's discuss your experience with taking risks, because this affects the way you start investing and building wealth.

Think about what actions feel risky to you: for example, skydiving, speaking in public, going on a date or travelling solo. These actions might feel very risky to some people, while to others they might be a piece of cake. This point is really important to reflect on; the same action can bring up a diverse range of viewpoints depending to who you speak to, their personal experiences and their knowledge of the topic. It's no different to investing. Many of our views are informed by the media, a family member's experience or misinformation from online forums. Have you historically considered investing to be a risky activity? Think about what you're basing these views on: your family history, past experiences, job and so on. The deeper you think about this, the better you'll understand your own risk profile and how that impacts the way you invest.

Managing risk as an investor

Sometimes we avoid taking the first step on our investing journey because of this concept of risk. No-one likes the idea of losing money, but is it possible to build wealth without taking on any risks? Sometimes people refer to products like savings accounts and term deposits as lower-risk options. But I'd argue that all financial decisions and products have an element of risk (or at least some degree of restriction) around them. Take a term deposit, for example. If your starting balance (capital) remains the same (always remember to read the fine print), but your rate of return (interest rate) is below inflation, you are actually losing purchasing power over time. Basically, $5 today won't buy as much in ten years' time. This is why many people still choose to invest, despite knowing that their investment may fall in value at some points along the way.

Is anything truly 'risk-free'?

It's important to be really careful with the idea of a 'risk-free' financial product. If someone comes up to me saying I'll get a risk-free return of 10 per cent a year on my money, warning bells sound in my head because investing involves the possibility that your investment will fall in value, and no-one can make a guarantee to you that it won't. This is often where people come unstuck on their money journey. If someone's promising you a certain return, saying you'll double your money in less than a year or offering you a stock they're certain will be the next big thing, this should stick out to you as a red flag.

Rather than looking for a risk-free option, I like to focus on ways I can reduce my risks as an investor and make my life calmer. (Getting stressed out about your investments is not going to help your happiness levels!) Let's work through some strategies for that now: not investing money you need in the short term, diversifying your portfolio, doing your research and understanding what's within your control.

Don't invest money you need in the short term

It's very important that you don't invest your emergency fund or any money you're putting away for short-term goals. The reason for this is that on any given day, month or year your investment could fall in value for reasons outside of your control (such as a global pandemic). Shares and ETFs are investments we typically make with a long-term view of 5–10 years at minimum. These investments need a long-term approach so they have time to grow.

One of the reasons investors lose money is that when their investment falls in value, they get scared and sell. However, if you go into investing with the understanding that there will be good years and bad years, you'll be more comfortable staying invested when you see your portfolio fall in value because you'll know it's all part of the journey.

Diversification is key

'Diversification' is a word that I think about a lot and in all areas of my life. I try to diversify my income streams, friendships, information sources, books, indoor plants and hobbies. It leads to a much richer (and happier) life in many cases, and it means if one thing falls through, I've still got a lot of options.

It's also a way that you can reduce the level of risk you take as an investor. You could use ETFs, shares, cash and bonds as the building blocks of your investment portfolio, for example. However, you might also like to research other investments, including those outside your home country and in different asset classes, like emerging markets and real estate, alongside investing in large global businesses.

There's a lot of data and research on building the ideal portfolio for your risk profile, age group and so on, but at the end of the day you need to build your portfolio around the life you want to live, accounting for all the things that make you unique. Remember, what your friend or Professor Google says to do won't necessarily be right for you and your individual circumstances. This is one of the reasons many people seek out personalised financial advice.

Do your own research

As an investor, it's important to have a good understanding of what you're buying. This gives you the confidence to make investment decisions and stick to your plan, even when you see headlines that say the market is falling. Use some of the research ideas in chapter 8 to get you started, and please don't invest in something you see advertised online if you can't explain to a friend what it does *at minimum*. There's a general rule of thumb that taking on more risk over a long period of time will lead to higher returns. However, if you invest in something without doing your homework and it turns out to be a poor investment, no amount of risk-taking can help you.

Control what you can – and know what you can't

In *Risk: A User's Guide*, General Stanley McChrystal writes that 'dealing with risk is the active practice of controlling every single factor within your reach'. You will never be able to control everything as an investor, so focus on managing the risks within your control.

So, how does all this tie into buying happiness? The more you understand the risks within your control and how to manage them, the less stressed you'll feel about investing. A lower-risk investment option may give you more peace of mind, for example. You need to invest in a way that lets you sleep at night.

Perhaps building a portfolio of shares you have to actively manage won't make you happy because the requisite research takes up too much of your time and the volatility of the market makes you nervous. You might instead decide that a hands-off approach to building your portfolio is better suited to your personality, and means you'll sleep a lot better at night. There's not often a conversation about designing your investment portfolio with your happiness in mind, but it's worth paying some thought to. On many occasions I've seen people create complex strategies that add nothing but headaches to their lives.

Finding the confidence to take healthy risks

The question then becomes, how do you take the right risks without being reckless, in your investing journey. This isn't an easy one to answer. Sometimes the choices you make will have lasting repercussions, and at other times it'll be easy to change your mind tomorrow.

If taking risks plays a role in our happiness and our journey to feeling financially independent (which we'll dive into in chapter 10), how do we overcome the fear of making the wrong decision? Here are a few strategies to try.

Find some control over the situation

What actions can you take to feel more in control of the situation? As a new investor, you're learning so many new things that it can be easy to feel overwhelmed. Focus on all the actions that are within your control, such as learning more about ETFs, putting some money aside to invest each month and investing small amounts on a regular basis. Remember, each action you take builds your confidence as an investor.

What are the facts?

Many of our fears are based on feelings and not facts. What is the worst-case scenario if you start investing? And what's the actual likelihood of that fear being realised? Do the research and find out. You can look at the historical performance of different investments – the S&P/ASX 200, for example – to see how the Australian share market has performed over the past few decades. Another helpful tool is the Vanguard Index Chart, which gives you a visual breakdown of how long-term investing works. Arming your brain with the facts and figures can often give you the confidence you need to take the first step.

Exposure therapy

It's time to get up close and personal with your fears. Can you find small ways to start investing and slowly increase the dosage, so to speak? This could provide you with a safe way to get comfortable with your fears around investing and encourage you to keep going. For some people, this might look like investing $5 through a micro-investing app, while for others it could look like investing with imaginary dollars using the ASX Sharemarket Game for a period. It could be good to find a close friend or family member to support you with this. Sometimes the act of taking the first step makes every step that follows easier.

Speak to an expert

Sometimes these things need a little bit of help to face, so this is where an expert counsellor or financial adviser could come in handy. If fear is holding you back from something you want to do (such as investing), speaking to an expert could really help.

✎ Some of the best parts of life happen just outside our comfort zone, so my challenge to you is to identify one thing you feel a little scared about when it comes to your money. Write down some steps you can take to face it and take action.

The biggest risk of all: Not doing anything

Sometimes what we need to overcome our fears around investing is the reminder that not getting started might be the biggest risk of all. Sure, if you don't invest, you might never directly experience the risk of loss and making a mistake, but you also might look back and wish you'd prioritised your financial future. As we discussed in chapter 8, the more time you give your investments to grow, the more you'll benefit from compound interest. Just think about how many more options you'll have in decades to come if you've built up a comfortable nest egg!

Making money mistakes

Before we jump into what to do if you make an error, let's break down a few of the most common money mistakes. I've already mentioned a few potential mistakes in my discussion of managing risk as an investor, such as investing money you need in the short term, forgetting to diversify and not doing your research, but here are a few more pitfalls you can avoid.

Investing based on emotions like fear or greed

One mistake we often make is making investment decisions based on strong emotions like fear or greed. These feelings can override our common-sense check and lead us astray. Building wealth doesn't happen overnight; it's often in chasing short-term returns where people come unstuck. You can overcome this by doing your research and writing down why an investment makes sense for you.

Looking too often at your performance

Now that you've opened up your brokerage account, it can be tempting to look at your investments daily (or even more often), but this can just create opportunities for mistakes. Even if you went into investing with a long-term approach, seeing your investments rising and falling in value can be unsettling at best and at worst trigger decisions based on emotion rather than reason. If you're struggling with this, remove your brokerage app from your phone, unsubscribe from financial news alerts and remind yourself why you started investing to begin with.

Giving up too soon

Long-term investing, which is what we've discussed in this book, only works when you let it. It's tempting to change your strategy at the first sign of trouble, but remember that the ups and downs of the share market is all part of the journey. Don't judge your investment based on its short-term performance. Remember to zoom out and look at the long-term performance. If you're feeling uncertain, remind yourself of the factors that are within your control (such as the amount you invest) and the factors outside your control (such as the economy).

But what if you make a mistake?

Okay, you made a mistake. So, what? To paraphrase the late Kobe Bryant, it's only a bad thing if you don't learn and grow from the experience. Sometimes you'll take a risk and it doesn't work out; that's what makes it a risk in the first place. Getting comfortable with making mistakes and learning from them is an important skill for investors. Even the experts make mistakes with their money, and

I want to stress that it shouldn't put you off getting back up and giving things another go.

Think of those big disclaimers on the front of financial products and podcasts saying *PAST PERFORMANCE IS NOT AN INDICATOR OF FUTURE PERFORMANCE.* It's very true in so many cases, and especially when it comes to your mistakes. If you learn from your mistakes, then you don't have to keep making similar mistakes in the future. For example, at the very beginning of my investing journey I invested in some companies I found online without doing any research. I lost some money from that experience, but it taught me crucial lessons: the importance of doing my own research, creating and sticking to a simple investing strategy and not to invest in things I don't understand.

Here are a few ideas to help you both learn and move on from mistakes. Let's use the common (and extremely relatable) example of investing in an Australian shares ETF, then getting nervous and selling a month later when the value of the investment fell. First, get some emotional distance. It's easy to dwell on mistakes, so do something to take your mind off everything and give your brain space to process. When you're ready to come back to the situation, spend some time reflecting on what caused the mistake and write down your observations. You might have invested before you were ready, not properly understood how the market works or felt scared watching your investment fall in value, for example. Now we're going to turn these reflections into lessons. What can you do to change the outcome next time you're in a similar position? You might realise from this process that you need to spend a bit more time learning about investing and getting comfortable with the idea that the market goes up and down. You could also decide that you're just too emotionally involved in the process and get the help of a professional, such as a financial adviser, to help you create a plan that's tailored to your goals. Finally, once you've reflected on your mistake and made a plan to move forwards, it's important to execute that plan and move on. Don't let one mistake stop you from working towards your financial goals.

Remember, you have more control over your financial future than you realise. By learning and growing from your money mistakes, you'll be well on your way to building wealth and buying happiness.

TL;DR

Taking risks is a big part of life, and it's something we need to get comfortable with as investors. In this chapter we unpacked how to manage the risks of investing to set ourselves up for success, push through the fear of getting started and avoid some common investing mistakes. In the next chapter we'll put together everything we've learnt so far and start turning investing skills into long-term financial freedom.

- It's important to understand your approach to taking risks so you can make more informed investing decisions.
- While all investing involves risk (the potential that your investment will fall in value), there are ways to manage this, including diversification and not investing money you need in the short term.
- Many new investors feel apprehensive about getting started, but this can be overcome by researching, taking tiny actions to build confidence and speaking to an expert.
- Mistakes are a normal part of investing and even the experts make them. The most important skill is to recognise and learn from them, and then get back up again.

10

Looking ahead

Becoming financially independent

My mom always says that when a woman is financially independent, she has the ability to live life on her own terms. I think that was the soundest advice that I ever got. No matter where you go in life or who you get married to, you have to be financially independent — whether you use it or not.
Priyanka Chopra

We've covered a lot of ground in this book, so what's next? In this chapter I want to talk about the feeling of being financially independent and what that could look like for you. We'll crunch some numbers and start to put together a plan; however, as you'll see, financial independence isn't necessarily about having millions of dollars. It's about having secure financial foundations, giving yourself more choice and making decisions about your life from a position of strength. After all, the more control and autonomy you have over your time, the happier you are. I'd argue if you can combine working towards financial independence with being satisfied with what you have right now, you're on a very good path to buying happiness.

What is financial independence?

Financial independence is more a feeling than a destination, though you may choose to attach a dollar figure to it. It doesn't mean you've reached all your goals; rather, it's a step in the process to buying happiness. This could look like having a full emergency fund, staying on top of your income and expenses each month and having a plan for how you're going to work towards your financial goals. As someone who has put some money aside for emergencies and knows their monthly numbers, I feel a sense of financial independence right now.

In *Work Optional*, Tanja Hester shares 'the profound joy that comes from creating a life that's uniquely yours', which she experienced on her own path to financial independence. When she sets goals for herself now, they have 'nothing to do with earnings or status or achievements'. Harvard psychologist Robert Waldinger would agree with her approach to goal-setting. He shared that we think (and are told by society) that 'fame, wealth and badges of achievement' will make us happy because 'they're measurable and quantifiable', but his long-running study of human happiness says otherwise.

That's the challenge. Being happy is about much more than the money, but money can solve a lot of our problems and give us more choice about how we spend our time. If we then invest our time in our relationships, we'll increase our long-term happiness levels.

Personally, I've set a big financial independence goal, which is for my investment portfolio to be large enough to cover my basic living costs. (Don't worry; we'll get to the numbers shortly.) This is my long-term financial goal and I'm not expecting to get there overnight. The big attraction of this goal for me is the feeling of empowerment and self-sufficiency financial independence can give. It's not necessarily about not having to work (although I may choose that at some point), but rather the ability to make choices from a position of strength, live life on my own terms and give back to my community.

Reaching financial independence is about working out what 'enough' means to you and then putting a financial plan in place to help you get there.

Why bother?

So, what *does* it mean to work towards and reach financial independence? At its core it's about consuming less, increasing your savings rate, investing the rest, finding satisfaction in the moment in front of you and having the financial freedom and flexibility to choose if, how and when you work. The details are totally up to you – and that's where it gets interesting.

People pursue financial independence for different reasons. For some it's an audacious goal to increase their freedom and choices in life, while for others it's about being able to take more time off work to care for family members. Here's a non-exhaustive list of some common motivations for pursuing financial independence:

- to take back control over one's time
- to have the confidence to leave a toxic or draining job
- to spend more time raising a family
- to provide full-time care for family
- to pursue passion projects permanently
- to volunteer or work in non-profits
- to ensure family is provided for
- to travel the world
- to start a business or work independently
- to focus more on health and wellbeing.

Do any of these resonate with you? Think back to the activities you completed earlier this book about designing your ideal day, writing down the things you'd love to do and creating some goals. Understanding your 'why' makes it much easier to create a plan that aligns with your values and figure out what you're working towards. Financial independence looks different to everyone. For some it might simply be having a full emergency fund. For others it's about having enough money to never rely on an employer again.

What does financial independence mean to you? What will motivate you to work towards that goal? Being able to answer these questions will help you keep going even when the path starts getting challenging. I personally pursue financial independence because I want to be in control of my time – more specifically, who I spend my time with, where I spend it and when. What I do want is for you to be aware of what money can do for you, and knowing your why behind investing and building wealth is important.

How much do I need?

For the purposes of this book, I'm going to look at the idea of financial independence that's discussed most, which is where someone's investments can support their living costs. This isn't to discount what I mentioned earlier in this chapter, but more to illustrate the numbers and reasoning behind a common goal. As we've already covered, this version of financial independence isn't going to be attractive to or possible for everyone; however, you'll be able to draw upon the principles to meet your own unique goals. Basically, we're turning our chapter 8 discussion about investing into something long-term and actionable. Whether you want to work towards building a $1,000 or $1,000,000 investment portfolio, it's important to have a plan, know the regular investments you need to make to get there, make decisions about how much you spend today and how much you put away for the future, and keep yourself accountable on the journey.

The most common aim of those targeting traditional financial independence is to have 25 times their annual cost of living invested in a diversified portfolio, with a safe annual withdrawal rate of 4 per cent. The intention is then to live off their investments indefinitely. Developed in the Trinity Study, this 4 per cent figure is commonly referred to as the safe withdrawal rate (SWR; please note that your SWR will differ slightly between countries and the asset classes you invest in). This guide isn't perfect, and according to Vanguard 'was originally designed for investors with a 30-year retirement horizon', not necessarily for early retirees with a timeframe of 50-plus years.

Let's break this down. If your investment portfolio is worth $1 million, and your SWR is 4 per cent, you could withdraw $40,000 from it every year to live on. If you're looking to retire on $100,000 a year, then your investment portfolio will need to be around $2.5 million to sustain that (4 per cent per year of $2.5 million is $100,000). Have a look at the different SWR studies out there and break down how much you spend each year on living costs. You're going to need to work out how much you need to comfortably live on each year. (Don't forget to include money for travel or kids if they're on the cards.) For this to work you need your money to be working hard for you. It needs to be invested in assets that are growing (like shares and ETFs).

If I'm happy to live off $40,000 per year, my financial-independence number could be around $1 million – and I'll therefore need to make a plan to reach that. In this scenario, it would take me approximately 20 years of investing $2000 a month to reach $1 million (if I'm assuming an average investment return of 7 per cent per year over the next 20 years, not accounting for fees and taxes). I highly recommend you start playing around with a compound-interest calculator to see how much you'll need to save and invest every year to achieve financial independence.

Financial independence and a long-term mindset

One of the really important ideas to understand if you're working towards a big investing goal is building a long-term mindset. This means you're setting goals that won't be achieved overnight. It can be difficult at the beginning to get your head around this idea; ten, 20 or even 30 years feels like an impossibly long time. One way to manage this is by creating small milestones along your journey and finding ways to enjoy the process. This could look like celebrating when you hit your first $1000, $10,000 and $100,000 invested and taking a moment to acknowledge how far you've come. It's not always easy. Some days it's awfully tempting to throw in the towel and just buy something extravagant, but when I feel like that I come back to my 'why' and remind myself what I'm working towards.

Remember: financial independence looks different for everyone, so my goals and milestones will be different to yours, which will be different to your friend's, which will be different to your colleague's, and so on. Personally, I want to build my portfolio to a point where I can support myself using both the income I receive from my investments and the capital growth (by selling small portions of my investments as needed). This is a big, long-term goal, but I'm also factoring smaller financial goals along the way, like buying a property, taking a mini-retirement and travelling.

To get you thinking about what's possible and what might suit your lifestyle and goals, here are some common milestones and goals you could include along your journey to financial independence:

- Understand your current financial picture by writing down all your assets and liabilities.
- Get out of debt as soon as possible by actively working on paying it down every month.
- Build an emergency fund to cover 3–6 months of living expenses in the event you're hit with unforeseen life events that affect you financially. (This is a crucial step on your path to becoming financially independent.)
- Create your new budget by reducing your expenses and focusing on putting a greater percentage of your income into your savings and investment accounts.
- Reduce your expenses and make considered purchasing decisions based on your values. This might include purchases that save you time or make you happier.

- Start a side hustle, take on extra shifts or up-skill yourself to increase your income so you can put more money towards your goals.
- Invest your first $5 using a micro-investing platform and start building up your confidence as an investor.
- 'Fun money' – you have enough money in your savings account or investment portfolio that you would be able to leave full-time work for a shorter period of time (for example, 12 months) to start a business, go travelling or work on a creative project.
- 'Part-time' – you have invested enough money to work just part-time or build a business instead of continuing full-time work. This could be funded through investment income or by selling a small portion of your investments if necessary to cover the reduction in your income.
- 'Financial independence' and beyond – your investment portfolio has reached a point where you can live off your investments indefinitely and live life on your own terms without having to work. Basically, you get to choose when, where and how you work now.

As you can see, financial independence isn't just about the end goal. By enjoying the process and celebrating your wins, your journey will be more sustainable in the longer term. As you plan out and continue on your money journey, remember that there's no one right way to reach financial independence or build your ideal life. Everyone's working it out as they go – just like you – based on their own values, priorities and life experiences.

✎ Before we dive into creating a plan, identify some of the milestones you could add to your journey to financial independence so you can regularly check in with and celebrate your progress.

What are you prepared to do?

If you've decided that financial independence is what you want to work towards, a key consideration is going to be your willingness to live your life differently to others so that you can reach your goals according to your own unique plan and timeframe. It goes without saying that you can't pull $1 million out of your hat.

Everyone's path towards financial independence looks different, but most people will have to make some changes to reach their goal. What could some of these changes look like? Here are some ideas:

- put solid financial habits in place, building an accountability system, making sure your income exceeds your expenses and knowing where your money is going
- prioritise putting more money towards investments (your future self) and less towards your present self
- find ways to cut down on big-ticket items (like expensive new cars)
- start a side hustle or get a second job so you have more money to invest
- invest in yourself so you can increase your income over time
- learn to cook well and cut down on takeaway and eating out (unless it brings you joy, that is)
- start buying more second-hand goods (rather than new) and get out of the consumerist mindset
- catch up with friends and family in less expensive ways (dinner party, picnic, camping, hiking, local travel and so on)
- move to an area with a lower cost of living so you can decrease housing and utility expenses.

✎ Have a think about what changes you could make in your life to make your financial independence goal a reality. To achieve big goals, you often have to make some big changes. Think about ways you can be more intentional with your spending.

As Melissa Browne wrote in *Unf*ck Your Finances*, 'What are you prepared to sacrifice?' There are always trade-offs. You're never going to be able to have and do everything you want at the same time. Deviating off the set path and instead working towards financial independence requires passion and perseverance, so it's important to understand why you're doing it. It comes back to knowing your 'why'. If you prioritise working towards financial independence, then the changes you make to get there don't feel as much like sacrifices.

Your unique investing plan

It's time to pull everything you've learnt about yourself, your goals and your finances together and make a plan. This process will build your confidence, allow you to consolidate everything you've learnt so far and help you to figure out what you still need to learn about. Keep this as simple as possible – and remember, it only needs to work for you.

Owen Rask, who works as an investment analyst, helped me put together this list of questions that'll really help you clarify your investment plan. Grab a piece of paper or open a Google Doc and jot down your responses to the following questions. You won't have all the answers right now, so come back to this list over time as you learn more about investing. Head to buyinghappiness.com.au to access a template for this.

Question 1: What is your long-term financial goal?

For example, you might want to build a million-dollar investment portfolio or have enough investment income to work only four days a week. Head back to our goal-setting discussion in chapter 2 if you need some guidance here. Take this opportunity to think about some of the smaller milestones you want to hit along the way, too.

Question 2: How will you reach that goal?

Use a compound interest calculator to work backwards. This will help you identify how much you need to invest each month and what your investment timeframe looks like (how many years you'll need to invest for to reach that goal). This will also tell you if your goal is a little far out of reach and some adjustments need to be made. For example, if I have a goal of investing $100,000 over five years, but I can only invest $5000 each year on my current income, I may need to reduce my goal, increase my timeframe or find additional income to invest.

Question 3: What will you invest in?

List the investments you'll make as part of your strategy (for example, ETFs, property, cash and so on). Then coming back to your personal tolerance for risk, write down what portion of your portfolio will be allocated to growth investments (such as shares) versus defensive investments (such as cash). If you're planning to invest in shares, consider articulating some rules to protect yourself, such as setting the maximum amount you'll invest in any one investment (for example, no more than 5 per cent of your investment portfolio can be in a single share.)

Question 4: Have you common-sense checked your expectations against reality?

Keep in mind that past performance doesn't guarantee future performance, but it does provide an indication of what could be realistic. Have a look at the Vanguard Index Chart and the long-term performance of your prospective investments to give your plan a dose of common sense and check it's realistic.

Question 5: What are the key risks that will stop you from achieving your goal?

Think of this as a 'pre-mortem'. Write down all the things that could stop you reaching your goal and find strategies to tackle each one, understanding that some things (like the economy) are outside of your control. In chapter 4 we covered the ways your brain can trick you. Now is the time to think about how you'll combat these behavioural biases before they become a problem for you.

Question 6: How will you make long-term progress towards your goal?

Finally, circling back to the second question, make sure you're clear on all the regular steps you'll take towards reaching your goals. Learning more about your finances will be an important part of this. Schedule a monthly check-in with your finances to keep yourself accountable. You can also consider how you'll track your portfolio's performance (for example, against the S&P 500), keep your financial admin up to date and make sure you're staying on top of any tax matters.

Your plan

These questions will take you some time to answer, but the ideas you write down here will come to form your plan. In fact, it took me years to fine-tune my own approach to investing – and I still don't always stick to the plan. That said, articulating your plan like this, getting it all written down, is a starting point and gives you confidence on your investing journey. Plus, it's a great document to modify over time as you learn more, come back to in times of investment volatility and use to record your journey. My suggestion is to keep coming back and refining your plan as you spend more time learning about yourself, your finances and how the world of investing works. Your plan doesn't need to be perfect. You can start small and learn as you go.

Don't stop here. I've included plenty of resources at the end of this book for you to keep learning from. Finally, if you're at all unsure about what you should be doing, remember that you can always talk to a financial adviser. There's no substitute that I can offer for the advice a professional can provide, tailored to your personal circumstances.

Building a life you love now

You don't need to wait to reach your money goals to start living your life. It's important to start building a life you love and enjoy – right now. That doesn't necessarily mean quitting your day job and going backpacking. Rather, it means spending your time and money in a more intentional way, putting joy into your life and making sure you don't build a life you desperately want to escape. Though you might be working hard to reach financial independence, don't neglect your family, friends, hobbies and personal goals. Yes, you may approach your finances and life differently now, but it shouldn't take away from the best parts of your life.

It's crucial to find a sustainable balance that allows you to make the most of the time you have now because you never know what's around the corner. As one of my all-time favourite humans Dolly Parton said, 'don't get so busy making a living that you forget to make a life'. Think about different ways you can make sure your financial goals don't take over your life so you can continue to enjoy the journey. Consider the following ideas, for example:

- taking mini retirements every few years
- travelling and working overseas
- working part-time, casually or as a contractor
- taking a pay cut so you can work closer to home without having to take work home
- starting a side hustle and focusing less on the corporate ladder.

Additionally, I highly recommend checking out Vicki Robin's classic *Your Money or Your Life*. Robin has a wonderful way of articulating the trade-offs we make daily and how our relationship with money is reflected in the sense of satisfaction and fulfilment that we get from our connections to family, community and planet. She says, 'the only real asset you have is your time, the hours of your life', which is a reminder to us all that there's a balance to everything – especially if we feel like we're getting caught up in our goals at the expense of our time.

Spending meaningfully and with intention

That balance is essential when it comes to spending money, too. Learning how to accumulate wealth is one part of the equation; the other part is learning how to spend meaningfully. As I've mentioned before, one of the interesting conundrums you'll face as you learn more about investing and the power of compound interest is balancing how much you spend right now and how much you save and invest to reach your future goals: for example, going on a $5000 holiday this year versus investing that money, knowing it could be worth nearly double that in just ten years.

The good news is that you can do both! You can:

- enjoy the moment while still looking after future-you
- invest in shares as well as property
- put money in your superannuation fund while also investing outside of it
- be career-focused and still go on a holiday.

It might just look a little different to how you first imagined because you won't necessarily be able to do it all at once. Behavioural finance expert Dr Daniel Crosby told me that one of the biggest challenges people face is the ongoing trade-off between enjoying today and securing tomorrow, which incidentally can cause a lot of tension in relationships. That's why it's so important to understand your priorities.

One way to strike the balance between spending and saving (and investing) on your journey to financial independence is to get a better understanding of *why* you're spending money and what value you'll get out of the purchase. The idea is not to never spend again if you're working towards financial independence. You're going to spend money for many different reasons and that's okay! It's a big part of your financial life. This strategy will just help you better make informed choices and negotiate trade-offs between spending, saving and investing money.

As this looks different to everyone, I've included in an appendix some examples of purchases that people in my community have gotten value and satisfaction out of. Buying happiness takes trial and error, so take the time to explore your relationship with money and how using it for present- and future-you feels. As you've probably gathered, finding the balance can be tricky (and it will change throughout your life), but being super clear on your goals and your plan for financial independence makes things a lot simpler. For example, if your goal is to invest $10,000 this year and you've done that, why should you second-guess that holiday with friends that'll provide you with meaningful experiences (that'll add joy to your life), strengthen your relationships (which is important for your happiness) and pay memory dividends for years to come (even better)?

TL;DR

Money can be used to buy time, happiness and choices, and it's possible over time to build your wealth to a level where you feel financially independent. The challenge can be figuring out what that looks like to you. So, take the time to really examine what your own goals are, how to add more choices into your life and what actions you can take today to ensure you're building a life you love right now – and a life that future-you will be proud of. You can use all the tools you've gathered from this book to kickstart your financial independence journey and start making confident money decisions right now.

- Reaching financial independence is all about consuming less, increasing your savings rate, investing the rest, finding satisfaction in the moment in front of you and having the financial freedom and flexibility to choose if, how and when you work.
- A common aim within those targeting financial independence is to have 25 times their annual cost of living invested in a diversified portfolio with a safe annual withdrawal rate of 4 per cent (so they can live off their investments indefinitely).

- Build your financial plan to reflect your own unique goals rather than taking a cookie-cutter approach. Build in flexibility to take time off to care for children, take a holiday or start a business if that's important to you.
- You'll spend money on your path to financial independence and that's okay! Just focus on making purchases with intention that will add happiness into your life today and that future-you will be proud of.

Conclusion

I've covered a lot of ground in this book, from laying financial foundations to building your own unique plan for financial independence. Before I conclude, I want to note some of the most important money lessons we've discussed over the last ten chapters. These are the key ideas that I'd love for you to take away, apply in your life and share with others:

- **Spend less than you earn.** This is one of the age-old rules of personal finance and will have a powerful impact over your lifetime. The earlier you can set up your finances so the money flowing into your bank account is greater than the money flowing out of it, the easier things will be.
- **Always have a get-out-of-jail-free card.** If you can, it's always a good idea to have spare money. From having back-up cash when travelling to maintaining a healthy emergency fund, make sure you're prepared for the challenges life throws at you.
- **Make your money work for you.** You work hard for your money, so make your money work hard for you. This might look like buying shares, buying property or making other types of investments through which your money can grow over time.
- **Spend your money intentionally.** As we've discussed, once you've identified what sorts of purchases make you happy, you can gain a lot of joy from your money. What brings you happiness will change throughout your life, so make it a habit to reassess your approach annually.

- **Talk about money.** Talking about money is important and these conversations have ripple effects. Challenge the narrative that money shouldn't be discussed and look for ways to initiate these conversations with friends and family.

What about happiness?

Despite everything you've read, you might still be wondering if any of what we've discussed is worth the trouble – whether getting your finances sorted, putting a budget in place and investing your first $5 is really going to make a difference in your life. You might even feel you're never going to have enough time, money, resources or knowledge to make a meaningful change to your financial future. And I get it. We've covered a lot of ground, and the claim that you can, to an extent, buy happiness, seems vague and hard to quantify. However, the research shows that the following statements are true for many people:

- There are ways you can spend your money to buy happiness.
- The better your relationships are, the better your life is.
- The more generously you give your time, the more time abundance you feel.
- The more willing you are to take risks, the higher your overall life satisfaction.
- When you donate money to others, you feel happier.

That said, for any of the concepts and strategies covered in this book to have even a chance of working, they have to be put into action. That means you need to experiment. Start by taking tiny steps in a positive direction.

An international panel of experts as part of the Blue Zones Happiness Consensus Project put together a list of the top ten strategies to improve wellbeing. Many of these strategies are mentioned in this book, including prioritising friends and family, getting involved in a community group, focusing on the happiness of others and making progress towards meaningful goals. The list also includes daily physical exercise, making a best friend at work and choosing the right spouse, which I haven't touched on. The point I'm making here is that there are a lot of factors that influence how satisfied you are with your life, outside of just your time and money, so learn as much as you can about what brings you happiness and satisfaction, and then incorporate those things into your life.

Remember, your personal finances are personal. It's easy to get caught up in comparing how you spend, save and invest your money with other people's habits, but you need to figure out what works for you and your unique situation. This is also where professional advice tailored to you and your goals can fit in perfectly. Just because it's popular wisdom doesn't mean it's right for you. Don't blindly copy someone. Your financial plan needs to be tailored to your life.

The power of small steps

I want you to commit to taking action now you've finished this book. I'm not talking about a drastic life makeover in 24 hours; I'm thinking instead of small, bite-sized goals that you've got no choice but to complete. The teacher of a writing program I completed a few years ago advised setting writing goals so small that they were almost ridiculous: waking up and writing for five minutes each day, for example. These five-minute writing bursts weren't going to produce a novel on their own. Rather, their purpose was to get me into the habit of showing up daily for myself. And five minutes turns into 20 minutes, turns into an hour, and so it goes.

This ethos is applicable here, too. Let me put it to you as a question: if you can't trust and rely on yourself for the tiny goals, what makes you think you'll turn up for those big goals? We need to build routine for ourselves in which we commit to turning up, even when it's hard.

We often set lofty goals for ourselves without building a sustainable framework that will enable us to achieve them. (I'm still working on this myself.) So this is my goal for you. Think of that thing that's been on your mind for a while that you still haven't completed. Have you got it? Now think about the smallest possible action you can take that will get you one tiny step closer to achieving that thing. Here are some examples:

- Want to sort out your spending? Start by writing down your last 24 hours of expenses.
- Want to start saving money? Transfer $5 into your savings account.
- Want to start investing? Open a micro-investing account and invest your first $5.

Are you laughing at how small your action seems? Good, you're doing it right. Could you repeat this small action every day for a week? Write the action down and put it somewhere obvious where you'll see it every single day (like the fridge). Once you master the art of showing up consistently for the small steps, you'll find it much easier to scale your goals up because you'll have proven to yourself that you can build powerful habits to change the direction of your financial future. The small choices you make each day have a compounding effect over time.

Take action now

This part is up to you. If you walk away from this book with no plan, chances are you'll look back in ten years and wonder why you didn't start earlier. The number one piece of advice I've received over the last seven years from experts around the globe is to get started *today*.

It's cliche to say that if nothing changes, nothing changes, but it's true. It'll feel hard and uncomfortable at times, but you need to start planting the seeds for your financial future today. Whether that's paying off debt or investing your first dollar, taking that first step is a crucial part of your journey. Once you're on the road, you can start experimenting with some of the ideas in this book for spending your time and money to buy happiness.

Ultimately the journey is yours, but it doesn't mean you're doing it alone. The more conversations we have about the tough subjects like money, the more we'll realise that we're all just figuring it out as we go along. Money touches every corner of our lives and, whether we like it or not, it's not going anywhere. So, find the places where money conversations are happening or be the person to start them.

An intentional life is built piece by piece, and it won't happen overnight, but you have more choices than you realise to change your financial future. Don't let anyone dissuade you from taking positive steps forward. Trust your gut. If it seems too good to be true, it probably is. The best way to build wealth and a life you love is with small actions taken lots of times. It's not a quick answer, but it's a realistic one.

In the appendices of this book, I'm going to share with you some inspiration for your journey. As a starting point, I've collected ways that listeners of the *Australian Finance Podcast* have bought happiness. Plus, in classic Kate fashion, I've also included some of my favourite books, websites and podcasts for you to explore. Find a topic that interests you, follow that thread and be curious. Life has a funny way of taking you in directions you never expected.

Remember, happiness isn't a destination. It's this moment in front of you, right now. Take hold of it with both hands and live.

[illegible] with some of [illegible] ideas [illegible] check [illegible]

[illegible]

[illegible] more conversations we have about the [illegible]

[illegible]

[illegible]

[illegible]

Crowdsourced happiness

In this appendix, I want to inspire you. It can be challenging to identify ways that you can spend your money and time to buy happiness, so I crowdsourced responses from my community to get you thinking. I've selected a few responses to each of my questions to show here, but I have much longer lists for you to explore at buyinghappiness.com.au – be sure to check them out and add your own ideas too!

First I asked my community for a material purchase they'd made recently that had increased their happiness levels. Here are some of their responses:

> *A hydro flask! The best investment I have made instead of wasting my money on bottles of water each time I go out.*

> *I've allowed myself the extra money to have all groceries and fruit/veg delivered. It's a game changer for a working mum of three children. Saves time and stress.*

> *A trampoline for my two-year-old daughter for her birthday. We spend hours on it together each week and have so much fun.*

> *Investing in braces. My family couldn't afford to take us to the dentist regularly and investing in straighter teeth as an adult is for me one of the best things I've bought for myself.*

> *This would hands down be my new camera. I want to document more of my life and to celebrate the people around me so I can*

look back in the future and be reminded of the small, happy, little moments.

Then I asked about experiential purchases they'd made recently that had increased their happiness levels. Here are some of the responses:

Camping trip to the Flinders Ranges. Takes 5 hours from Adelaide (in Australia), so expensive with petrol, and though the booking fees aren't too expensive it does all add up. Despite spending time and money getting there, being in nature makes such a difference in my happiness levels.

My gym membership! I train at a low-cost gym up front for 12 months and making it a priority to go. Getting my butt there makes me feel accomplished regularly as juggling life outside of work is a constant challenge.

A dog. We were putting it off due to costs, but we made room in the budget as it was companionship my partner and I wanted for a while.

A beginner's pottery class with my daughter. We spent time together, had a laugh, learnt a new skill and came home with some bowls we can now use to remember the experience.

I also asked what they think has been the lowest-cost activity or purchase that has had the greatest impact on their happiness. Given we're facing rising living costs and many of us have cut back on our spending, I want to push you to think about those lower-cost parts of your life that still have a big impact on your happiness. This is what they said:

Meeting in the park with friends so that our little ones can run around and we can catch up.

Going for a walk with my mentor at work. The walking part is free, but occasionally we grab a coffee. I look forward to this every fortnight.

Buying a serve of hot chips!

Enrolling my son in swimming lessons and watching his face light up when he gets in the pool.

Friday night dinner with friends. We always eat in, taking it in turns to cook. We all look forward to hanging out on Friday nights in the comfort of our homes – no Ubers, no expensive drinks. It's the highlight of my week.

It's funny; so much generic personal finance advice talks about cutting out your daily coffee in favour of saving or investing the money. However, both purchased and homemade coffees with family, friends and colleagues came up time and time again in the responses I collected. So, I wanted to leave this individual's response with you:

I began going to my local coffee shop for a coffee early in the morning when I couldn't sleep and I became friends with the owner. He now employs my daughter. He introduced me to a whole group of people that are part of my community. This helped improve my happiness as I had recently been widowed. Two years later, there are many in that circle that I would call friends.

Given the happiness-boosting properties of investing in our relationships, I also asked my community what the best thing they've spent money on for someone else was. Here's what they said:

A gift after one of my friends' mums had passed away from cancer –a well-deserved massage treatment.

Without a doubt, buying my daughter a puppy when she turned 11 was the best thing I've ever spent money on. She still has moments when she stops and is amazed by the fact that she now lives with an affectionate little creature that she can love and look after.

I'm a comedian and I donate $1 per ticket from my shows to local women's charities. I like feeling the show is making a difference in the real world.

Tickets for Mum to see her favourite band, which she couldn't have purchased herself.

A new TV for my Nonna, who couldn't afford one herself and had an old quality one. In her old age, watching TV is one of the things she spends the most time doing. What's the point of money if you can't use it to help others who have helped you in your life?

Finally, let's flip this around and have a look at some of the most rewarding ways we can spend our time, because that's an important part of the equation. Here's what my community had to say:

Practising music and yoga with YouTube (no cost at all).

Walks through nature and near the beach, sometimes on my own or with my partner. It's free, the scenery is stunning, fresh air, seeing the different variety of plants, insects and animals. It really clears my head and gives me the opportunity to appreciate the natural beauty of Australia.

Gardening is the most rewarding way I feel I spend my time. Feels like my investment strategy when I get a grown plant and graft it to start smaller new plants. Patiently waiting for them to compound like my investments. I know they don't feel like much at the beginning, but slowly my house and investments are growing like a tropical forest.

I am an avid traveller and always enjoy finding low-cost ways of having high-quality experiences, and I also love my 'mini retirements' when I take 3–12 months off work to slow down, reconnect with myself, family and friends, and give myself time to reflect, learn and change direction to stay true to who I am now and who I want to become.

As you can see, there are so many unique ways that people are already using their time and money to buy happiness. Now it's time to focus on you. Take everything you've learnt from this book, pieces of inspiration from these lists and everything you know about yourself and what makes you happy – and start experimenting.

You get to make choices in your life that will have a huge impact on your overall wellbeing. You just need to make the decision to start. It's not always easy, but it's definitely worth it! If you want to read more of these responses and share your own, head to buyinghappiness.com.au.

Acknowledgements

Nothing we do exists in a vacuum, so I want to thank those individuals who have supported me throughout my journey and played a role in both my life and the creation of this book.

Firstly, to Susan, my mother. You encouraged me to take risks in my life from an early age, and that has given me the confidence to build the life I have right now. Thank you for helping me grow into the strong, financially independent woman I am today.

To my father, David. Thank you for your endless love and support, alongside many delicious meals and cups of tea.

To my sister, Margaret. You've always been a great cheerleader in my corner, and I'm so glad you've started investing early on in your life.

To my wonderful podcast co-host, Owen. From that first conversation on Twitter in 2018, you've changed my life, and I couldn't be more grateful for everything you've taught me.

To my friends, Monique, Max, Ivy, Laura and many others. Thank you for all your early feedback on the book and for entertaining these conversations with me over the years.

To the Major Street Publishing team. You have been invaluable throughout this process and a huge supporter of the podcast over the years. Thank you, Lesley, Eleanor, Lauren, Will and everyone else!

This book is where I'm at right now at this point in my life. It's not perfect, but it's real, and it covers some of the most pressing questions my community have asked over the last seven years as well as research from experts around the world. Plus, it gives you plenty of ideas to kickstart your own personal finance journey. It's important to remember there's no one right answer to money questions and, at the end of the day, you need to own your financial future.

About the author

Kate Campbell is a financial educator who loves talking to anyone who will listen about one of the most taboo (and important) topics: money. You can find her writing articles on personal finance, creating free online courses at Rask Education (on everything from budgeting to financial independence) and speaking at events. If it's got something to do with personal finance, Kate's involved.

Kate has previously worked at Citigroup, InvestSMART and Timelio, and she cut her teeth on multiple financial operations and investment administration roles in the industry. She holds a Bachelor of Business Management from the University of Canberra and has completed General Advice, Managed Funds, Superannuation and Securities RG146 qualifications with Kaplan Professional.

Kate also hosts the *Australian Finance Podcast*, one of Australia's top-ranking finance podcasts.

Resources

For an extended list of resources, visit buyinghappiness.com.au.

Books

Finance

The Barefoot Investor: The Only Money Guide You'll Ever Need, Scott Pape

The Behavioral Investor, Daniel Crosby

Die with Zero: Getting All You Can from Your Money and Your Life, Bill Perkins

Happy Money: The Science of Happier Spending, Elizabeth Dunn and Michael Norton

How to Decide: Simple Tools for Making Better Choices, Annie Duke

The Psychology of Money: Timeless Lessons on Wealth, Greed, and Happiness, Morgan Housel

Sort Your Career Out: And Make More Money, Shelley Johnson and Glen James

*Unf*ck Your Finances*, Melissa Browne

Work Optional: Retire Early the Non-Penny-Pinching Way, Tanja Hester

Your Money or Your Life: 9 Steps to Transforming Your Relationship with Money and Achieving Financial Independence, Vicki Robin

Life and happiness

Atomic Habits: Tiny Changes, Remarkable Results, James Clear

The Blue Zones of Happiness: Lessons from the World's Happiest People, Dan Buettner

Eight Dates: Essential Conversations for a Lifetime of Love, John Gottman and Julie Gottman

Flourish: The Extraordinary Journey into Finding Your Best Self, Antonia Case

Four Thousand Weeks: Time Management for Mortals, Oliver Burkeman

The Good Life: And How to Live It, Robert Waldinger and Marc Schulz

Happiness: A Very Short Introduction, Dan Haybron

The Happiness of Pursuit: Finding the Quest That Will Bring Purpose to Your Life, Chris Guillebeau

How to Live: 27 Conflicting Answers and One Weird Conclusion, Derek Sivers

The Paradox of Choice: Why More is Less, Barry Schwartz

Other helpful resources

Australia-specific podcasts

Aussie Firebug

Australian Finance Podcast (my podcast)

The Broke Generation

Equity Mates Investing Podcast

my millennial money

She's on the Money

You're in Good Company

Global podcasts

Afford Anything

Deep Dive with Ali Abdaal

Invest Like the Best with Patrick O'Shaughnessy

The Money with Katie Show

The Morgan Housel Podcast

Standard Deviations

The Tim Ferriss Show

Websites

Australian Securities Exchange (ASX; asx.com.au): Use this website to look up different investments, access education resources and for the share market game.

Australian Taxation Office (ATO; ato.gov.au): This website has helpful guides on everything you need to know about tax in Australia.

MoneySmart (moneysmart.gov.au): Run by ASIC, this website provides a helpful overview of everything to do with personal finances and investing, alongside helpful tools like the compound interest calculator.

Rask Education (education.rask.com.au): Find free financial education courses on budgeting, investing, property, superannuation and more at this website.

Vanguard Australia (vanguard.com.au): This website hosts helpful resources on investing, including the Vanguard Index Charts.

Additional support

National Debt Helpline (ndh.org.au)

Financial Rights Legal Centre (financialrights.org.au)

Gambling Help Online (gamblinghelponline.org.au)

References

Introduction

Australian Psychological Society, 'Australian loneliness report', *Australian Psychological Society*, 2018. <researchbank.swinburne.edu.au/file/c1d9cd16-ddbe-417f-bbc4-3d499e95bdec/1/2018-australian_loneliness_report.pdf>

Australian Psychology Society, 'Loneliness', *Australian Psychology Society*, n.d. <psychology.org.au/for-the-public/psychology-topics/loneliness>

Capital Group, 'Confronting the money taboo', *Wisdom of Experience: Investor survey series*, December 2018. <capitalgroup.com/content/dam/cgc/shared-content/documents/reports/MFGEWP-062-1218O.pdf>

A Case, *Flourish: The Extraordinary Journey Into Finding Your Best Self*, Bloomsbury Continuum, 2023.

DM Haybron, *Happiness: A Very Short Introduction*, Oxford University Press, 2013.

Chapter 1 | Finding your feet: Pay off high-interest debt and build your emergency fund

afterpay, 'Supercharge sales. Get new customers', *afterpay*, n.d. <afterpay.com/en-au/business>

Financial Counselling Australia, *National Debt Helpline*, n.d. <ndh.org.au/>

Financial Rights, *Financial Rights Legal Centre*, n.d. <financialrights.org.au/>

Klarna, 'Boost your business with Klarna', *Klarna*, n.d. <klarna.com/au/business/>

moneysmart, 'Credit card calculator', moneysmart, n.d. <moneysmart.gov.au/credit-cards/credit-card-calculator>

GA Selgin, 'Commercial banks', *Britannica*, 30 June 2023. <britannica.com/topic/bank/Commercial-banks>

Chapter 3 | Building your money mindset: Unpack your story, manage financial regrets and overcome limiting money beliefs

P Brickman, D Coates & R Janoff-Bulman, 'Lottery winners and accident victims: Is happiness relative?', *Journal of Personality and Social Psychology*, vol. 36, no. 8, pp. 917–927, 1978. <doi.org/10.1037/0022-3514.36.8.917>

K Campbell & O Rask, '1 lifestyle hack for 2023 (Owen's vision board activity)', *Rask Media*, 3 February 2023. <raskmedia.com.au/2023/02/03/1-lifestyle-hack-for-2023-owens-vision-board-activity/>

J Clear, *Atomic Habits*, Random House UK, 2018.

S Hankins, M Hoekstra & PA Skiba, 'The ticket to easy street? The financial consequences of winning the lottery', *The Review of Economics and Statistics*, vol. 93, no. 3, 2017. <jstor.org/stable/23016088>

AJ Hess, 'Here's why lottery winners go broke', *CNBC*, 25 August 2017. <cnbc.com/2017/08/25/heres-why-lottery-winners-go-broke.html>

CL Harter & JFR Harter, 'The link between adverse childhood experiences and financial security in adulthood', *Journal of Family and Economic Issues*, vol. 43, no. 4, pp. 832–842, 2022. <doi.org/10.1007/s10834-021-09796-y>

World Economic Forum, *The Future of Capital Markets: Democratization of Retail Investing In collaboration with Accenture and BNY Mellon*, World Economic Forum, 4 August 2022. <www3.weforum.org/docs/WEF_Future_of_Capital_Markets_2022.pdf>

Chapter 4 | Hack your brain: Overcome common behavioural traps including the fear of making a mistake and analysis paralysis

The Decision Lab, 'Why do we buy insurance? Loss-aversion, explained', *The Decision Lab*, n.d. <thedecisionlab.com/biases/loss-aversion>

SS Iyengar & MR Lepper, 'When choice is demotivating: Can one desire too much of a good thing?', *Journal of Personality and Social Psychology*, vol. 79, no. 6, pp. 995–1006, 2000. <doi.org/10.1037/0022-3514.79.6.995>

B Schwartz, *The Paradox of Choice: Why More Is Less*, HarperCollins Publishers, 2016.

R Sethi, 'How to live a rich life (+rules that will help you ACHIEVE it!)', *I Will Teach You To Be Rich*, 27 February 2023. <iwillteachyoutoberich.com/how-to-live-a-rich-life/>

H Stead & PA Bibby, 'Personality, fear of missing out and problematic internet use and their relationship to subjective well-being', *Computers in Human Behavior*, vol. 76, pp. 534–540, 2017. <doi.org/10.1016/j.chb.2017.08.016>

A Tandon, A Dhir, I Almugren, GN AlNemer & M Mäntymäki, 'Fear of missing out (FoMO) among social media users: a systematic literature review, synthesis and framework for future research', *Internet Research*, vol. 31, no. 3, pp. 782–821, 2021. <doi.org/10.1108/INTR-11-2019-0455>

Chapter 5 | Money talks: Have good conversations about money with people in your community

American Psychological Association, '2022 Stress in America', *American Psychological Association*, October 2022. <apa.org/news/press/releases/stress/2022/october-2022-questions.pdf>

American Psychological Association, 'Happy couples: How to avoid money arguments: With practice, partners can learn to talk about finances in a healthier, more satisfying way', *American Psychological Association*, 2015. <apa.org/topics/money/conflict>

J Dew, S Britt & S Huston, 'Examining the relationship between financial issues and divorce', *Family Relations*, vol. 61, no. 4, pp. 615–628, 2012. <doi.org/10.1111/j.1741-3729.2012.00715.x>

JJ Gladstone, JM Jachimowicz, AE Greenberg & AD Galinsky, 'Financial shame spirals: How shame intensifies financial hardship', *Organizational Behavior and Human Decision Processes*, vol. 167, pp. 42–56, 2021. < doi.org/10.1016/j.obhdp.2021.06.002>

J Gottman & JS Gottman, *Eight Dates: Essential Conversations for a Lifetime of Love*, Workman Publishing, 2019

The Harris Poll, 'October 2022 topline data', *American Psychological Association*, October 2022. <apa.org/news/press/releases/stress/2022/october-2022-topline-data.pdf>

K Little, 'Survey: Lending cash to loved ones ends badly for nearly half of Americans', *Bankrate*, 26 September 2019. <bankrate.com/finance/credit-cards/lending-money-survey-2019>

S Pape, *The Barefoot Investor*, Wiley, 2016.

LM Vowels, KB Carnelley & RRR Francois-Walcott, 'Successful negotiation of goal conflict between romantic partners predicts better goal outcomes during COVID-19: A mixed methods study', *Journal of Social and Personal Relationships*, vol. 39, no. 2, pp. 155–178, 2022. <doi.org/10.1177/02654075211033341>

Chapter 6 | Spend your time better: Enjoy the present while investing in the future

D Ballas & D Dorling, 'Measuring the impact of major life events upon happiness', *International Journal of Epidemiology*, vol. 36, no. 6, 2007. <doi.org/10.1093/ije/dym182>

O Burkeman, *Four Thousand Weeks: Time Management for Mortals*, Vintage, 2022.

K Campbell, 'How to: audit your life, make hard decisions & prioritise your own happiness', *Australian Finance Podcast*, Rask Media, 26 April 2023. <raskmedia.com.au/2023/04/26/audit-your-life-make-hard-decisions-prioritise-your-happiness/>

K Campbell & O Rask, 'Invest your time better with Nir Eyal', *Australian Finance Podcast*, Rask Media, 27 February 2022. <raskmedia.com.au/2022/02/28/time-vs-money-take-control-of-your-life-with-nir-eyal/>

N Eyal, *Indistractable: How to Control Your Attention and Choose Your Life*, Benbella Books, 2019.

C Guillebeau, *The Happiness of Pursuit: Find the Quest that will Bring Purpose to Your Life*, Macmillan.

Harvard Second Generation Study, *Welcome to the Harvard Study of Adult Development*, n.d. <adultdevelopmentstudy.org/>

H Hershfield, *Your Future Self: How to Make Tomorrow Better Today*, Piatkus, 2023.

HE Hershfield, DG Goldstein, WF Sharpe, J Fox, L Yeykelis, LL Carstensen & JN Bailenson, 'Increasing saving behavior through age-progressed renderings of the future self', *Journal of Marketing Research*, vol. 48, pp. S23–S37, 2011. < doi.org/10.1509/jmkr.48.SPL.S23>

R Larson, 'Is Feeling "in Control" Related to Happiness in Daily Life?', *Psychological Reports*, vol. 64, no. 3, 1989. <doi.org/10.2466/pr0.1989.64.3.775>

Merriam-Webster Dictionary, 'Affluence', *Merriam-Webster Dictionary*, n.d. <merriam-webster.com/dictionary/affluence>

W Mischel, EB Ebbesen & A Raskoff Zeiss, 'Cognitive and attentional mechanisms in delay of gratification', *Journal of Personality and Social Psychology*, vol. 21, no. 2, pp. 204–218, 1972. <doi.org/10.1037/h0032198>

C Mogilner, 'You'll feel less rushed if you give time away', *Harvard Business Review*, September 2012. <hbr.org/2012/09/youll-feel-less-rushed-if-you-give-time-away>

C Mogilner, Z Chance & MI Norton, 'Giving time gives you time', *Psychological Science*, vol. 23, no. 10, pp. 1233–1238, 2012. <doi.org/10.1177/0956797612442551>

C Newport, *Digital Minimalism*, Penguin, 2020.

GA Pignatiello, RJ Martin & RL Hickman, 'Decision fatigue: A conceptual analysis', *Journal of Health Psychology*, vol. 25, no. 1, pp. 123–135, 2020. <doi.org/10.1177/1359105318763510>

D Pink, *The Power of Regret: How Looking Backward Moves Us Forward*, A&U, 2022.

MEP Seligman, *Flourish: A Visionary New Understanding of Happiness and Well-being*, Atria, 7 February 2012.

D Sivers, *Hell Yeah or No: What's Worth Doing*, Sivers Inc, 2022.

J Sollisch, 'The cure for decision fatigue', *Wall Street Journal*, 10 June 2016. <wsj.com/articles/the-cure-for-decision-fatigue-1465596928>

Statista, 'Daily time spent on social networking by internet users worldwide from 2012 to 2023', *Statista*, 2023. <statista.com/statistics/433871/daily-social-media-usage-worldwide/>

B Ware, *The Top Five Regrets of the Dying*, Hay House, 2012.

A Whillans, 'Exchanging cents for seconds: The happiness benefits of choosing time over money' [thesis], *University of British Columbia*, 2017. <open.library.ubc.ca/collections/ubctheses/24/items/1.0348134>

Chapter 7 | Buying happiness: Maximise your enjoyment of life

S Allen, *The Science of Generosity*, Greater Good Science Centre, May 2028.

M Blanding, 'More proof that money can buy happiness (or a life with less stress)', *Harvard Business School Working Knowledge*, 25 January 2022. <hbswk.hbs.edu/item/more-proof-that-money-can-buy-happiness>

H Burns, 'How you can use anticipation to enjoy life more,' *The New York Times*, 31 May 2022. <nytimes.com/2022/05/31/well/mind/anticipation-happiness.html>

PA Caprariello & HT Reis, 'To do or to have, or to share? Valuing experiences over material possessions depends on the involvement of others', *Journal of Personality and Social Psychology*, vol. 104, no. 2, pp. 199–215, 2013. <doi.org/10.1037/a0030953>

E Diener & MEP Seligman, 'Very happy people', *Psychological Science*, vol. 13, no. 1, 81–84, 2002. <doi.org/10.1111/1467-9280.00415>

E Dunn & M Norton, 'How to Make Giving Feel Good', *Greater Good Magazine*, 18 June 2013. <greatergood.berkeley.edu/article/item/how_to_make_giving_feel_good>

EW Dunn, DT Gilbert & TD Wilson, 'If money doesn't make you happy, then you probably aren't spending it right', *Journal of Consumer Psychology*, vol. 21, no. 2, pp. 115 – 125, 2011. <doi.org/10.1016/j.jcps.2011.02.002>

L Entis, 'How to spend money to squeeze more joy out of life', Vox, 20 November 2019. <vox.com/the-highlight/2019/11/13/20951937/money-experiences-buy-happiness-happy-how-to-spend>

JM Jachimowicz, EL Frey, SC Matz, BF Jeronimus & AD Galinsky, 'The sharp spikes of poverty: Financial scarcity is related to higher levels of distress intensity in daily life', *Social Psychological and Personality Science*, vol. 13, no. 8, pp. 1187–1198, 2022. <doi.org/10.1177/19485506211060115>

A Kumar, MA Killingsworth & T Gilovich, 'Waiting for merlot: Anticipatory consumption of experiential and material purchases', *Psychological Science*, vol. 25, no. 10, pp. 1924–1931, 2014. <doi.org/10.1177/0956797614546556>

The Life You Can Save, 'What we do', *The Life You Can Save*, n.d. <thelifeyoucansave.org>

A Mogensen, 'Giving without sacrifice? The relationship between income, happiness, and giving' [manuscript], n.d. <assets.ctfassets.net/dhpcfh1bs3p6/3jqEdXNDmg8SGAeOeC8KYo/63f9caa4de752b15c84455dc9025d537/giving-without-sacrifice.pdf>

SS Monfort, HE Stroup & CE Waugh, 'The impact of anticipating positive events on responses to stress', *Journal of Experimental Social Psychology*, vol. 58, pp. 11–22, 2015. <doi.org/10.1016/j.jesp.2014.12.003>

M Norton, 'How to buy happiness', *TED*, 25 April 2012. <ted.com/talks/michael_norton_how_to_buy_happiness>

B Perkins, *Die With Zero: Getting All You Can from Your Money and Your Life*, HarperCollins Publishers, 2021.

Psychology Today, 'Hedonic treadmill', *Psychology Today*, n.d. <psychologytoday.com/us/basics/hedonic-treadmill>

Chapter 8 | From little things big things grow: Understand compound interest, start investing and automate your financial future

Australian Institute of Health and Welfare, 'Gambling in Australia', *Australian Institute of Health and Welfare*, 16 September 2021. <aihw.gov.au/reports/australias-welfare/gambling>

Australian Gambling Research Centre, *Gambling participation, experience of harm and community views: An overview*, Australian Institute of Family Studies, March 2023. <aifs.gov.au/sites/default/files/2023-03/2302-overview_gambling-participation-harm-views.pdf>

moneysmart, 'Compound interest calculator', *moneysmart*, n.d. <https://moneysmart.gov.au/budgeting/compound-interest-calculator>

SD Simpson, 'A Brief History of Exchange-Traded Funds', *Investopedia*, 31 January 2022. <investopedia.com/articles/exchangetradedfunds/12/brief-history-exchange-traded-funds.asp>

Statista, 'Number of exchange traded funds (ETFs) worldwide from 2003 to 2022', *Statista*, 2023. <statista.com/statistics/278249/global-number-of-etfs/#:~:text=There%20were%208%2C754%20ETFs%20globally,almost%2010%20trillion%20U.S.%20dollars>

Chapter 9 | Nothing ventured, nothing gained: Taking risks and making mistakes

AC Brooks, 'The magic of a little danger: To get happier, be brave, not reckless', *The Atlantic*, 7 July 2022. <theatlantic.com/family/archive/2022/07/how-to-take-smart-risks/661487/>

ASX, 'Sharemarket game', *ASX*, n.d. <asx.com.au/investors/investment-tools-and-resources/sharemarket-game>

T Dohmen, A Falk, D Huffman, U Sunde, J Schupp & GG Wagner, 'Individual risk attitudes: New evidence from a large, representative, experimentally-validated survey', *IZA discussion papers*, no. 1730, September 2005. <docs.iza.org/dp1730.pdf>

C Guven, 'Reversing the question. Does happiness affect individual economic behavior? Evidence from surveys from the Netherlands and Germany' [job market paper], *University of Houston*, 2007. <uh.edu/~cguven/papers/CAHITGUVEN_JOBMARKETPAPER.pdf>

S Hareli, S Elkabetz, Y Hanoch & U Hess, 'Social perception of risk-taking willingness as a function of expressions of emotions', *Frontiers in Psychology*, vol. 12, no, 655314, 2021. <doi: 10.3389/fpsyg.2021.655314>

D Hryshko, MJ Luengo-Prado & BE Sørensen, 'Childhood determinants of risk aversion: The long shadow of compulsory education', *Quantitative Economics*, vol. 2, no. 1, pp. 37–72, 2011. <doi.org/10.3982/QE2>

S McChrystal, *Risk: A User's Guide*, Penguin, 2023.

Chapter 10 | Looking ahead: Becoming financially independent

S Bartlett, 'E246: 7 Life-changing lessons from the longest ever study on health & happiness! Dr. Robert Waldinger', *Diary Of A CEO*, 11 May 2023. <open.spotify.com/episode/6koDsVabKQZiT2aMkLB2zP>

M Browne, *Unf*ck Your Finances*, Orion, 2021.

P Costa, D Pakula & AS Clarke, 'Fuel for the F.I.R.E.: Updating the 4% rule for early retirees', *Vanguard*, June 2021. <corporate.vanguard.com/content/dam/corp/research/pdf/Fuel-for-the-F.I.R.E.-Updating-the-4-rule-for-early-retirees-US-ISGFIRE_062021_Online.pdf>

T Hester, *Work Optional: Retire Early the Non-Penny-Pinching Way*, Hachette, 2019.

A Marjolin, K Muir, M Weier, I Ramia, A Powell, R Reeve, C Connolly, F Salignac & K-A Ho, 'Financial resilience in Australia', *Centre for Social Impact*, December 2018. <csi.edu.au/research/financial-resilience-in-australia/>

V Robin, *Your Money or Your Life*, Penguin, 2008.

R Waldinger & M Schulz, *The Good Life: Lessons from the World's Longest Study on Happiness*, Random House, 2023.